America's Flat-Out Ass-Kickin' Rock 'n' Roll TV Show

PETER CHECKSFIELD

FOR HEATHER

CONTENTS

INTRODUCTION

A few years back, the Ultimate Classic Rock website published an article on ABC TV's 'Shindig!', calling it "Flat-Out, Ass-Kickin' Rock 'n' Roll TV" - and they weren't exaggerating! You don't believe it? Well, apart from the fact that the show featured up to a hour of non-stop music and (mostly) live performances, let's have a quick look at just a few of the 300+ artists who appeared on the show during its all too brief 16 month run from September 1964 to January 1966...

There's **Rock 'n' Roll** (Chuck Berry, Little Richard, Jerry Lee Lewis, Bo Diddley, The Everly Brothers, The Coasters); **British Invasion** (The Beatles, The Rolling Stones, The Who, The Kinks, Manfred Man, The Dave Clark Five, The Hollies, The Yardbirds, The Zombies, The Pretty Things); **US Groups & Duos** (The Byrds, The Beach Boys, The Turtles, The Lovin' Spoonful, The Kingsmen, The Sir Douglas Quintet, The Righteous Brothers, Sonny & Cher); **Soul** (James Brown, Tina Turner, Marvin Gaye, Jackie Wilson, Aretha Franklin, Ray Charles, The Isley Brothers, Sam Cooke, The Temptations); **Girl Groups** (The Shangri-Las, The Ronettes, The Blossoms, The Ikettes, The Angels, The Dixie Cups, The Supremes, The Chiffons); **Solo Artists** (Roy Orbison, Charlie Rich, P.J. Proby, Gene Pitney, Donovan, Lesley Gore, Sandie Shaw, Jackie DeShannon, Marianne Faithfull, Cilla Black), even **Blues** (Howlin' Wolf, Jimmy Witherspoon) and **Country** (Johnny Cash, Hank Williams Jr.).

NO other '60s TV show could boast such a cool list of acts, not the UK's 'Ready, Steady, Go!', 'Thank Your Lucky Stars' and 'Top Of The Pops', and certainly not American rival shows 'Hullabaloo', 'Shivaree' or 'Hollywood A Go-Go'.

In this book, I look at *every* artist and their songs in *every* episode, from its tentative Pilot shows, through its ground-breaking peak, to the show's dramatic and swift demise. With over 500 screen-shots, mini-bios, US and UK chart positions, anecdotes, trivia and more, this really is the first and last word on America's Flat-Out Ass-Kickin' Rock 'n' Roll TV Show!

Peter Checksfield

www.peterchecksfield.com

- Jack Good, an Englishman famed for the UK's 'Oh, Boy!', 'Wham!' and 'Boy Meets Girls', created and initially produced the show. He quit after 30th June 1965, when Director Dean Whitmore took over.

- There were 3 "Pilot" and/or rejected shows prior to the series starting proper.

- It ran from 16th September 1964 to 8th January 1966 on the US ABC Network.

- The show's main presenter was Jimmy O'Neill, a Los Angeles DJ who was married to songwriter Sharon Sheeley.

- Whilst the vast majority of performances featured live vocals, they often used pre-recorded instrumental backing tracks.

- Episodes 1 - 19 (16th September 1965 - 13th January 1965) = 1 x 30 minute episode per week.

- Episodes 20 - 51 (20th January 1965 - 8th September 1965) = 1 x 60 minute episode per week.

- Episodes 52 - 85 (16th September 1965 - 8th January 1966) = 2 x 30 minute episodes per week.

- 'Shindig!' was a victim of its own success in that it quickly inspired other look-a-like (but inferior) TV shows such as 'Hullabaloo' (NBC), 'Shivaree' (ABC) and 'Hollywood A Go-Go' (CBS).

- In October 1965, it was announced that 'Shindig!' was to be cancelled. There was then a notable decline in quality and, sometimes, a change of format for many of the remaining episodes.

- The show was spoofed in a December 1965 episode of 'The Flintstones', with the TV show called 'Shinrock!', hosted by 'Jimmy O'Neillstone' and featuring 'The Beau Brummelstones'.

- There have never been any rebroadcasts of 'Shindig!' shows in full. However, Rhino Home Video released a series of VHS compilations in the early '90s.

- The first two Pilots aren't available for viewing at time of writing, but every subsequent episode was fully viewed and reviewed for this book.

- Some of the "screen shots" in this book are in less-than-perfect quality and have the presence of on-screen time counters, but they still give a good idea of visual content (a few individual clips circulate in greater quality, but for the sake of consistency I've used the same source for each episode).

*** = denotes performances that were taped in London.**

JIMMY O'NEILL AND JACK GOOD. WITHOUT WHOM …

1st Pilot: 'Young America Swings The World', Taped 2nd February 1963

Jackie DeShannon - Sing Sing Sing
P.J. Proby - Endless Sleep + Turn Me Loose
The Chambers Brothers, **Clydie King** and **The Sweet Things** - Peppermint Twist + What'd I Say
Tura Johnson - Personality
Scooter Teague - Mack The Knife
Also appearing: **Jesse Collins**, **The Chaps**, **The Young America Girls**, **The Leon Russell Band**, **Glen Campbell** and **David Gates.**

Exact order of performances unconfirmed!

JACKIE DESHANNON: Sharon Lee Myers (b. 1941). Singer and songwriter from Hazel, Kentucky. She'd only had limited success up to now, despite a recording career that dates back to 1956, but would go on to greater things in the coming months and years. Jackie DeShannon would appear on 5 Episodes of 'Shindig!', including the very last show on 8th January 1966.

P.J. PROBY: James Marcus Smith (b. 1938). Rhythm 'n' Blues and Pop singer from Houston, Texas. P.J. Proby had been releasing singles under this name since 1961 and prior to that under the name 'Jett Powers', but success had so far eluded him. Despite this, Jack Good obviously believed in him, as P.J. was featured in both this show, the 2nd Pilot, and 2 broadcast 'Shindig!' Episodes, as well as the UK Jack Good produced 'Around The Beatles' TV special which launched his successful UK career. 'Endless Sleep' is the only song from this show that is currently available for viewing, and the performance is a strange one: His singing is fine, but it is also a rather stilted performance, with an unsmiling P.J. Proby standing motionless, with none of the flamboyance that he would soon be famous for.

THE CHAMBERS BROTHERS: Willie Chambers (b. 1938 - guitar and vocals), (b. 1942 - guitar and vocals), George Chambers (b. 1931 - d. 2019 - bass and vocals), Lester Chambers (b. 1940 - harmonica and vocals) and Brian Keenan (b. 1943 - d. 1985 - drums). Soul and Folk group from Carthage, Mississippi, best known for their 1968 No.11 hit 'Time Has Come Today'. The Chambers Brothers later appeared in 4 more Episodes of 'Shindig!'.

CLYDIE KING: Clydie May Crittendon (b. 1943 - d. 2019). Soul singer from Dallas, Texas. Clydie King was later renown for her session work. She would also feature in 'Shindig!' Episode 39.

THE SWEET THINGS: Francine Hurd (Francine Hurd Barker, b. 1947 - d. 2005), Dyanne Stewart and Nancy J. Johnson. Soul group from Washington DC. Released singles with and without Clydie King.

TURA JOHNSON: Tura Johnson was an obscure singer of Swedish origin, despite her rendition of Lloyd Price's 'Personality' being in Italian. She never appeared in a regular edition of 'Shindig!'.

SCOOTER TEAGUE: Edwin Ardell Teague (b. 1940 - d. 1989). Actor and dancer from Jacksboro, Texas, perhaps best remembered for his role in 1961's 'West Side Story'. In common with Tura Johnson, he never appeared in a proper 'Shindig!' Episode.

DAVID GATES: David Ashworth Gates (b. 1940). Country and Pop singer and guitarist from Tulsa, Oklahoma. David Gates had been releasing singles since 1957, but it wouldn't be until the early '70s with the band Bread that he'd find major success.

2nd Pilot: Shindig! - Taped 17th January 1964 / Broadcast 9th May 1964

Johnny Cash - Bad News + Dark As A Dungeon
Roy Clark - Cowboy Boots
Roy Clark and **The Eligibles** - Alabama Jubilee
Roy Clark and **The Wellingtons** - God Did A Wonderful Thing
Roy Clark and **The Collins Kids** - I'm Movin' On + Oh, Lonesome Me + Y'all Come
The Collins Kids - Night Train To Memphis
Chris Crosby - Honeycomb
P.J. Proby - Cumberland Gap + Rock Island Line + Hitchhike To Georgia
Dodie Stevens - Jambalaya

Exact order of performances unconfirmed!

JOHNNY CASH: John R. Cash (b. 1932 - d. 2003). Country, Rockabilly and Folk singer and guitarist from Kingsland, Arkansas. 'Bad News' and 'Dark As A Dungeon' were both B-sides of 1964 singles. He would also appear in 'Shindig!' Episode 19.

ROY CLARK: Roy Linwood Clark (b. 1933 - d. 2018). Country singer and guitarist from Meherrin, Virginia. The host for this Pilot Episode, he would also appear in 'Shindig!' Episodes 26 and 46.

THE ELIGIBLES: Stan Farber, Ron Hicklin, Ron Rolla and Bob Zwirn. Pop vocal group from Renton, Washington. They appeared on the show a further 7 times.

THE WELLINGTONS: Kirby Johnson, Ed Wade and George Patterson. Folk vocal trio from Urbana, Illinois. Very much 'Shindig!' regulars, they appeared on the show another 33 times.

THE COLLINS KIDS: Lawrencine 'Lorrie' Collins (b. 1940 - d. 2018) and Lawrence 'Larry' Collins (b. 1942). Rockabilly and Country duo from Creek County, Oklahoma. They would later appear in 'Shindig!' Episode 51.

CHRIS CROSBY: Christopher Harry Crosby. Pop singer from Los Angeles, California. Bing Crosby's nephew, Chris Crosby would also appear on 'Shindig!' Episode 7.

P.J. PROBY: Although none of these songs were ever released by P.J. Proby on record, 'Cumberland Gap' and 'The Rock Island Line' were performed as a medley on 'Around The Beatles', a Jack Good produced UK TV special that was taped at London's IBC Studios on 28th April 1964, and broadcast on 6th May 1964.

DODIE STEVENS: Geraldine Ann Pasquale (b. 1946). Pop singer from Chicago, Illinois. Best known for her 1959 No. 3 hit 'Pink Shoe Laces', she never appeared on any other 'Shindig!' Episode.

3rd Pilot: Shindig! - Taped 11th July 1964

Although generally referred to as a Pilot show, 'Shindig!' had already been commissioned by the time of its taping, therefore making this in fact more of a rejected Episode #1.

Opening Medley: **Delaney Bramlett** and **The Angels** - Tom Dooley / **The Blossoms** - Don't Hang Up / **Pat and Lolly Vegas** - Hard Day's Night / **Hollywood All Stars** and **The Blossoms** - Shout / **The Righteous Brothers** - Shout + (Up Above My Head) There's Music In The Air / **Little Richard** - Joy, Joy, Joy (End of Medley)

The Hollywood All Stars - Jamaica Ska

The Righteous Brothers - Little Latin Lupe Lu

Jody Miller - Saved

Delaney Bramlett - Gamblin' Man

The Angels - Chapel Of Love

Pat and Lolly Vegas - Medley: La Bamba - Twist and Shout

Delaney Bramlett - Memphis

The Blossoms - (I Do The) Shimmy Shimmy

Righteous Brothers - Ko Ko Joe

Little Richard - Bama Lama Bama Loo + Whole Lotta Shakin' Going On

THE RIGHTEOUS BROTHERS: Bill Medley (William Thomas Medley, b. 1940) and Bobby Hatfield (Robert Lee Hatfield, b. 1940 - d. 2003). Rhythm 'n' Blues and Pop duo from Orange County, California. More than any other performers, The Righteous Brothers owe their success to 'Shindig!', appearing on the show a mammoth 26 times. 'Little Latin Lupe Lu' was the duo's debut single and 1st hit, peaking at No. 49 in the US charts.

JODY MILLER: Myrna Joy Miller (b. 1941). Country and Pop singer from Phoenix, Arizona. As well as this Pilot, she appeared on 4 broadcast Episodes of 'Shindig!'.

THE ANGELS: Peggy Santiglia (Peggy Santiglia Ricker, b. 1944), Phyllis Allbut (Phyllis Allbut Sirico, b. 1942) and Barbara Allbut (Barbara Allbut Brown, b. 1940). Girl Group from New Jersey. Best remembered for their 1963 US chart-topper 'My Boyfriend's Back', by 1964 their career was in decline, despite releasing a single entitled 'Little Beatle Boy'! They never appeared on any broadcast Episodes of 'Shindig!', but their performance of 'Chapel Of Love' is excellent.

PAT AND LOLLY VEGAS: Patrick Vasquez (b. 1941 - vocals and bass) and Lolly Vasquez (b. 1939 - d. 2010 - vocals and guitar). Soul and Pop duo from Fresno, California. Later members of Native American band Redbone, they would also appear in Episode #23.

LITTLE RICHARD: Richard Wayne Penniman (b. 1932 - d. 2020). Rock 'n' Roll, Rhythm 'n' Blues, Gospel and Soul singer and pianist from Macon, Georgia. 'Bama Lama Bama Loo' was his first hit since a return to rock 'n' roll after several years recording gospel music, peaking at No. 82 in both the US Pop and R&B charts, and it did a little better in the UK at No. 20. With Richard jumping on top of the piano during the finale and stirring the audience into a frenzy, rock 'n' roll TV doesn't get any better than this. It was all a bit too much for ABC TV executives though, who demanded something a little more suitable for family viewing. Little Richard never appeared on a broadcast 'Shindig!' Episode.

SHINDIG!

L-R: The Blossoms; The Righteous Brothers; Jody Miller; The Angels; Delaney Bramlett; Little Richard

Episode 1: 16th September 1964

Opening Medley: **Jackie and Gayle** - (Up Above My Head) There's Music In The Air / **The Wellingtons** and **The Blossoms** - Yes, Indeed / **Jackie and Gayle** - Gonna Build A Mountain / **Jackie and Gayle**, **The Righteous Brothers** and **The Everly Brothers** - (Up Above My Head) There's Music In The Air (reprise)

Shindig Dancers (singing to picture of **Bobby Sherman**) - If I Had A Talking Picture Of You

Bobby Sherman - Back Home Again In Indiana

The Wellingtons - Tzena, Tzena, Tzena

Jackie and Gayle - The Girl From Ipanema

Sam Cooke - Tennessee Waltz

The Everly Brothers - You're The One I Love

Donna Loren - Wishin' and Hopin'

The Righteous Brothers - This Little Girl Of Mine

Alan Sues (Liberace impersonation)

Bobby Sherman - Hello Dolly (Duet with 'Shindig!' dancer Maria Ghava)

The Everly Brothers - Hi-Lili, Hi-Lo

Sam Cooke - Blowing In The Wind

Alan Sues (another Liberace impersonation)

The Everly Brothers and **Sam Cooke** - Lucille

THE SHINDIG DANCERS: A dancing (and occasionally singing) troupe that appeared on most editions of the show, members include Diane Stuart, Pam Freeman, Gina Trikinis, Carole Shelyne, Marianna Pecora, Teri Robinson, Laurine Yarnell, Virginia Justus, Maria Gavha and Rini Jarmon.

BOBBY SHERMAN: Robert Cabot Sherman Jr. (b. 1943). Pop singer and Actor from Santa Monica, California. Very much a regular, he appeared on the show 43 times.

SAM COOKE: Samuel Cook (b. 1931 - d. 1964). Rhythm 'n' Blues, Soul, Pop and Gospel singer from Clarksdale, Mississippi. 'Tennessee Waltz' was the B-side of his No. 11 hit 'Good Times', reaching No. 35 in its own right. His inspired performance of 'Blowing In The Wind' is a strong candidate for the finest ever Sam Cooke footage.

THE EVERLY BROTHERS: Don Everly (Isaac Donald Everly, b. 1937) and Phil Everly (Phillip Everly, b. 1939 - d. 2014). Rock 'n' Roll and Country duo from Muhlenberg County, Kentucky. 'You're The One I Love' was their latest single which didn't chart, 'Hi-Lili, Hi-Lo' is from the 1961 'Both Sides Of An Evening' album, and their 1960 revival of Little Richard's 'Lucille' got to No. 21 in the US and No. 4 in the UK. This is the first of 8 'Shindig!' appearances.

DONNA LOREN: Donna Zukor (b. 1947). Pop singer and Actress from Boston, Massachusetts. Another 'Shindig!' regular, she appeared on the show 27 times.

ALAN SUES: Alan Grigsby Sues (b. 1926 - d. 2011). Comedian from Ross, California, later best known for his recurring roles in 'Rowan and Martin's Laugh-In'.

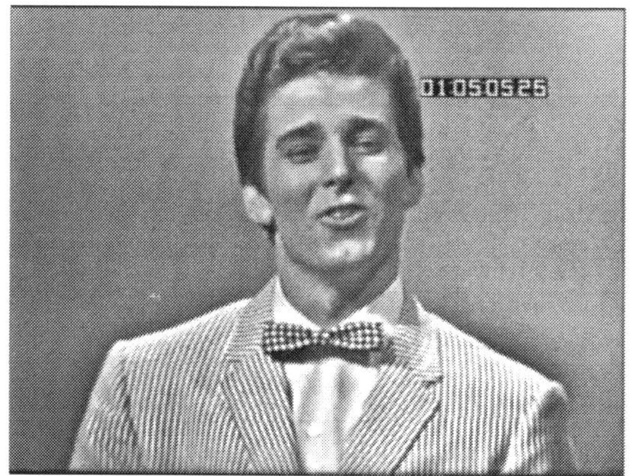

L-R: Bobby Sherman; Jackie and Gayle; Sam Cooke; Donna Loren; The Everly Brothers; The Everly Brothers and Sam Cooke

Episode 2: 23rd September 1964

Opening Medley: **Alan Sues**, **Jerry Cole** - Ain't She Sweet? / **The Cables** and **The Blossoms** - Cannon Ball / **The Righteous Brothers**, **Jody Miller** and **Pamela Bennett** - California Here I Come (End of Medley)

Jody Miller - Yes, My Darling Daughter

The Righteous Brothers - Ko Ko Joe

Pamela Bennett - And I Love Him

Alan Sues - Put Your Arms Around Me, Honey

Bobby Freeman - C'Mon and Swim

The Righteous Brothers - My Babe

Delaney Bramlett - You Never Can Tell

Darlene Love - You'll Never Get To Heaven (If You Break My Heart)

The Cables - Way Down Yonder In New Orleans

Johnny Rivers - Maybelline + Memphis

Jody Miller - Saved

THE BLOSSOMS: Darlene Love (Darlene Wright, b. 1941), Fanita James (Fanita Barrett) and Jean King (d. 1983). Pop and Soul trio from Los Angeles, California. Although they were recording artists in their own right, The Blossoms are best remembered for being the actual group who sang on The Crystals' 'He's A Rebel', as well as prolific backing vocalists. They appeared on more than 50 Episodes of 'Shindig!'. Darlene Love also made 3 solo appearances on the show, as did Jean King, while Fanita James got solo billing just once. Darlene's performance of Dionne Warwick's 'You'll Never Get To Heaven (If You Break My Heart)' is one of this show's highlights.

PAMELA BENNETT: Seen here performing a rather shrill version of The Beatles' classic, little more is known about her.

BOBBY FREEMAN: Robert Thomas Freeman (b. 1940 - d. 2017). Rhythm 'n' Blues and Soul singer from Alameda County, California. 'C'mon and Swim' was a No. 5 US hit.

THE RIGHTEOUS BROTHERS: Their 2nd single, 'My Babe' peaked at No. 75.

DELANEY BRAMLETT: Delaine Alvin Bramlett (b. 1939 - d. 2008). Rhythm 'n' Blues, Country and Gospel singer and guitarist from Pontotoc, Mississippi. He appeared as a solo artist on 8 'Shindig!' Episodes as well as the 3rd Pilot show, and many more times as a member of The Shindogs.

JOHNNY RIVERS: John Henry Ramistella (b. 1942). Rock 'n' Roll, Pop and Country singer and guitarist from Baton Rouge, Louisiana. Both songs are somewhat subdued revivals of Chuck Berry songs, and both were successful singles with 'Maybelline' a US No. 12 and 'Memphis' a US No. 2.

JODY MILLER: 'Saved' is a Leiber and Stoller song that was a minor hit for LaVern Baker in 1960.

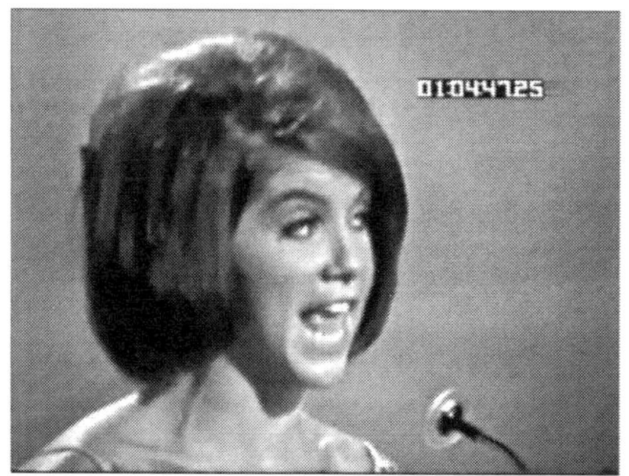

L-R: Jody Miller; The Righteous Brothers; Pamela Bennett; Bobby Freeman; Darlene Love; Johnny Rivers

Episode 3: 30th September 1964

Jackie and Gayle, The Newbeats and The Walker Brothers - He's Got The Whole World In His Hands

The Walker Brothers - Slow Down

The Blossoms - Tell Him

Gale Garnett - We'll Sing In The Sunshine

Jerry Cole - Oh, Pretty Woman

The Newbeats - Bread and Butter

John Bill - House Of The Rising Sun

Jackie and Gayle - A Summer Song

The Walker Brothers - Do Wah Diddy Diddy

Bobby Sherman - Have I The Right?

Donna Loren - It's Alright

Round Robin - The Roundest Of Them All

THE WALKER BROTHERS: Scott Walker (Noel Scott Engel, b. 1943 - b 2019 - vocals and bass) and John Walker (John Joseph Maus, b. 1943 - d. 2011 - bass and vocals). Pop duo from Los Angeles, California, who would find far greater success when dropping their instruments, adding drummer Gary Walker (Gary Leeds, b. 1942) and relocating to the UK. This is the first of 2 'Shindig!' appearances. Unlike on their later hits, it is very much John Walker who dominates, particularly on 'Do Wah Diddy Diddy'.

THE BLOSSOMS: Although a bit fast, their version of The Exciters' 'Tell Him' is a show highlight.

GALE GARNETT: Gale Zoë Garnett (b. 1942). Folk singer from Canada who was born in New Zealand. 'We'll Sing In The Sunshine' was a No. 4 US hit. She would make 1 further appearance on the show.

JERRY COLE: Jerald Edward Kolbrak (b. 1939 - d. 2008). Session guitarist and occasional singer from Green Bay, Wisconsin. Judging by his vocal on 'Oh, Pretty Woman', he was a far better guitarist than vocalist.

THE NEWBEATS: Larry Henley (Joel Henley, b. 1937 - d. 2014), Dean Mathis (Louis Aldine Mathis, b. 1939, Hahira, Georgia) and Mark Mathis (Marcus Felton Mathis, b. 1942). Vocal group from Shreveport, Louisiana. 'Bread and Butter' was their biggest hit, getting to No. 2 in the US charts, as well as No. 15 in the UK. The group would make 2 more appearances on the show.

JOHN BILL: A solo acoustic performance, little more is known about this Folk singer and guitarist.

JACKIE AND GAYLE: Jacqueline Miller (b. 1937) and Gayle Caldwell (b. 1941 - d. 2009). Pop and Folk Duo. Former members of The New Christy Minstrels, Jackie and Gayle were semi-regulars, appearing on the show 10 times.

ROUND ROBIN: Robin Lloyd. Soul and Pop singer from Los Angeles, California. A sort of fatter Chubby Checker, his fun single 'The Roundest Of Them All' was not a hit.

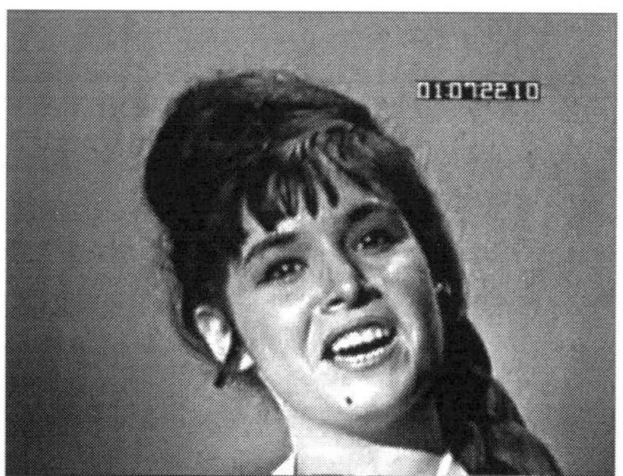

L-R: The Walker Brothers; Gale Garnett; The Newbeats; John Bill; Jackie and Gayle; Round Robin

Episode 4: 7th October 1964

The Beatles - Kansas City/Hey! Hey! Hey! Hey! *

The Karl Denver Trio - Wimoweh *

Lyn Cornell - Fever *

Tommy Quickly - Stagger Lee *

Sandie Shaw - (There's) Always Something There To Remind Me *

Sounds Incorporated - Sounds Like Locomotion *

P.J. Proby - You'll Never Walk Alone + Hold Me *

The Beatles - I'm A Loser + Boys *

Karl Denver - Old Folks At Home *

THE BEATLES: John Lennon (John Winston Lennon, b. 1940 - d. 1980 - vocals, guitar and harmonica), Paul McCartney (James Paul McCartney, b. 1942 - vocals and bass), George Harrison (b. 1943 - d. 2001 - guitar and vocals) and Ringo Starr (Richard Starkey, b. 1940 - drums and occasional vocals). Beat Group from Liverpool, UK. 'Kansas City/Hey! Hey! Hey! Hey!' is from the UK 'Beatles For Sale' and the US 'Beatles VI', 'I'm A Loser is from 'Beatles For Sale' and the US 'Beatles '65', and the Ringo-sang cover of The Shirelles 'Boys' dates back to the 1963 UK 'Please Please Me' album and the US 'Introducing The Beatles'. This excellent 3-song live performance was taped especially for 'Shindig!' in London's Granville Theatre on 3rd October 1964. The first two songs hadn't been released at the time of the broadcast ('Kansas City/Hey! Hey! Hey! Hey!' hadn't even been *recorded* yet), so they were a real scoop for the show.

THE KARL DENVER TRIO: Karl Denver (Angus Murdo McKenzie, b. 1931 - d. 1998 - vocals and guitar), Kevin Paul (Kevin Paul Neil - guitar) and Gerry Cottrell (Gerald Cottrell - bass). Folk and Country Trio from Manchester, UK. 'Wimoweh' was a UK No. 4 hit in 1962. 'Old Folks Home' (a 19th Century Stephen Foster song also known as 'Swanee') makes a very anti-climatic finale.

LYN CORNELL: (B. 1940). Pop singer from Liverpool, UK. A former member of vocal group The Vernons Girls, Lyn was married to session drummer Andy White - who played drums on the UK single version of The Beatles' 'Love Me Do'.

TOMMY QUICKLY: Thomas Quigley (b. 1945). Pop and Beat singer from Liverpool, UK. The first of 2 appearances.

SANDIE SHAW: Sandra Ann Goodrich (b. 1947). Pop singer from Dagenham, Essex, UK. Sandie Shaw's debut hit, this peaked at No. 52 in the USA and topped the charts in the UK. She would appear in a total of 6 'Shindig!' Episodes.

SOUNDS INCORPORATED: Alan 'Boots' Holmes (b. 1940 - saxophone and flute), 'Major' Griff West (David Glyde, b. 1940 - saxophone and flute), Barrie Cameron (Barrie Cameron-Elmes, b. 1939 - saxophone and organ), John St. John (John Gillard, b. 1940 - guitar), Wes Hunter (Richard Thomas, b. 1941 - bass) and Tony Newman (Richard Anthony Newman, b. 1943 drums). Mainly Instrumental Rock 'n' Roll and Beat Group from Dartford, Kent, UK. The first of 2 performances on the show, 'Sounds Like Locomotion' was a 1962 single.

P.J. PROBY: P.J. Proby's 1st single following his introduction to the UK via the 1964 'Around The Beatles' TV spectacular, 'Hold Me' was also his biggest UK hit at No.3. In complete contrast to his subdued performance of 'Endless Sleep' in the first Pilot show, here he is gloriously over the top.

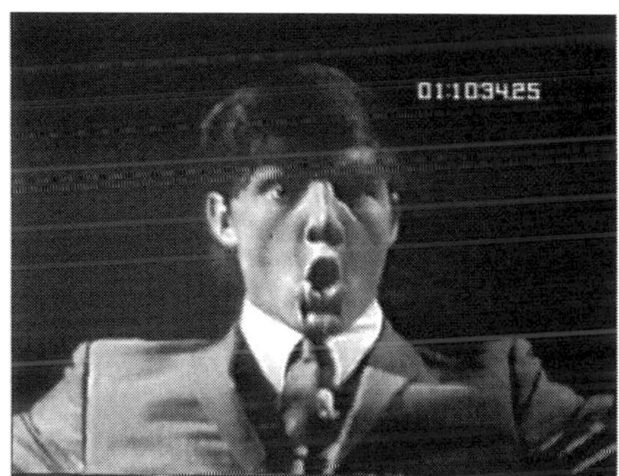

L-R: The Beatles; The Karl Denver Trio; Lyn Cornell; Tommy Quickly; Sandie Shaw; P.J. Proby

Episode 5: 14th October 1964

Adam Faith - It's Alright

Manfred Mann - Do Wah Diddy Diddy *

Bobby Sherman - You Make Me Happy

Elkie Brooks - Nothing Left To Do But Cry *

Roy Orbison - Oh, Pretty Woman

The Hondells - Little Honda

Adam Faith - Big Time

The Everly Brothers - Let It Be Me

The Everly Brothers - Gone, Gone, Gone

Roy Orbison - What'd I Say?

ADAM FAITH: Terence Nelhams Wright (b. 1940 - d. 2003). Rock 'n' Roll and Pop singer from Acton, London, UK. A big star in the UK where he had 24 hits during 1959-1966, 'It's Alright' wasn't one of them: an uptempo US-only single, it was his biggest American hit at No. 31. This is the first of 7 'Shindig!' appearances.

MANFRED MANN: Manfred Mann (Manfred Sepse Lubowitz, b. 1940 - keyboards), Paul Jones (Paul Pond, b. 1942 - vocals and harmonica), Mike Vickers (b. 1940 - guitar, alto sax and flute), Tom McGuinness (Thomas John Patrick McGuinness, b. 1941 - bass and guitar) and Mike Hugg (Michael John Hugg, b. 1942 - drums and vibes). Rhythm 'n' Blues and Pop group from London, UK. 'Do Wah Diddy Diddy' topped the charts in both the US and UK. This is the first of 7 'Shindig!' appearances.

ELKIE BROOKS: Elaine Bookbinder (b. 1945). Rhythm 'n' Blues and Pop singer from Salford, Lancashire, UK. Later a big star in her homeland, 'Nothing Left To Do But Cry' was the A-side of her 2nd single. This is the first of 2 'Shindig!' appearances.

ROY ORBISON: Roy Kelton Orbison (b. 1936 - d. 1988). Pop, Rockabilly and Country singer and guitarist from Vernon, Texas. 'Oh, Pretty Woman' topped the charts in both the US and UK.

THE HONDELLS: Jerry LeMire (vocals and guitar), Ritchie Burns (Richard Burns, d. 2010 - vocals and bass), Randy Thomas (Randy Steven Thomas, B. 1944 - keyboards and vocals) and Wayne Edwards (drums). Surf and Pop band from Los Angeles, California. 'Little Honda' was a US No. 9 hit. This first of 2 'Shindig!' appearances, 'Little Honda' features actress Teri Garr among the dancers on the back of the mopeds.

THE EVERLY BROTHERS: 1959's 'Let It Be Me' was a US No. 7 and UK No. 13 hit, and their latest single 'Gone, Gone, Gone' reached US No. 31 and UK No. 36.

L-R: Adam Faith; Manfred Mann; Elkie Brooks; Roy Orbison; The Hondells; The Everly Brothers

Episode 6: 21st October 1964

Donna Loren - Down The Line
Willy Nelson - Jump Back
Jackie Wilson - She's All Right
Bobby Sherman - Man Overboard
The Blossoms - Dancing In The Street
Bobby Sherman with **The Chambers Brothers** - I'm Crying
Donna Loren - That's What Love Is Made Of
Jay and The Americans - Come A Little Bit Closer
The Righteous Brothers - Let The Good Times Roll
The Honeycombs - Have I The Right? *
Jackie Wilson - Baby Workout

DONNA LOREN: 'Down The Line' was a Jerry Lee Lewis B-side, and this performance features Leon Russell doing his best on piano.

WILLY NELSON. (b. 1944). Pop singer from Teaneck, New Jersey. Not to be confused with country singer Willie Nelson, he was the cousin of Rick Nelson. This is the first of 9 'Shindig!' appearances.

JACKIE WILSON: Jack Leroy Wilson Jr. (b. 1934 - d. 1984). Rhythm 'n' Blues and Soul singer from Detroit, Michigan. His latest single, 'She's All Right' was a US Pop No. 102 and R&B No. 39, and 1963's 'Baby Workout' a US Pop No. 5 and R&B No. 1. This is the first of 4 'Shindig!' appearances.

THE BLOSSOMS: As on so many 'Shindig!' episodes, The Blossoms almost steal the show, this time with a fine cover of Martha and The Vandellas' 'Dancing In The Street'.

DONNA LOREN: Another regular who was always good value, here she performs The Miracles' 'That's What Love Is Made Of'.

JAY AND THE AMERICANS: Jay Black (David Blatt, b. 1938 - vocals), Sandy Deane (Sandy Yaguda - vocals), Howie Kane (Howard Kirschenbaum - vocals) and Marty Sanders (Martin Joseph Kupersmith - vocals and guitar). Pop group from Queens, New York. 'Come A Little Closer' got to No. 3 in the US charts. This is the first of 3 'Shindig!' appearances.

THE RIGHTEOUS BROTHERS: 'Let The Good Times Roll' is a good version of the Shirley and Lee song that was also revived by The Animals.

THE HONEYCOMBS: Denis D'Ell (Denis James Dalziel, b. 1943 - d. 2005 - vocals), Allan Ward (b. 1945 - guitar), Martin Murray (b. 1941 - guitar), John Lantree (John David Lantree, b. 1940 - bass) and Honey Lantree (Anne Margot Lantree, b. 1943 - d. 2018 - drums and occasional vocals). Beat Group from London, UK. 'Have I The Right?' got to No. 5 in the US charts and was a chart-topper in the UK.

L-R: Willy Nelson; Jackie Wilson; Bobby Sherman; Donna Loren; Jay and The Americans; The Honeycombs

Episode 7: 28th October 1964

Billy J. Kramer with The Dakotas - Da Doo Ron Ron
Leon Russell - Hi-Heel Sneakers
Dick and Dee Dee - Freight Train
The Blossoms - Baby Love
Chris Crosby - The Glory Of Love
Dick and Dee Dee - Thou Shalt Not Steal
The Wellingtons - For All We Know
Bobby Sherman - You Really Got Me
Billy J. Kramer with The Dakotas - Little Children
Billy J. Kramer with The Dakotas - From A Window
Billy J. Kramer with The Dakotas - Great Balls Of Fire

BILLY J. KRAMER AND THE DAKOTAS: Billy J. Kramer (William Howard Ashton, b. 1943 - vocals), Mick Green (Michael Robert Green, b. 1944 - d. 2010 - guitar), Mike Maxfield (b. 1944 - guitar), Robin MacDonald (bass) and Tony Mansfield (Anthony Bookbinder, b. 1943 - drums). Beat singer from Liverpool and Beat Group from Manchester. 'Little Children' was a US No. 7 and a UK No. 1, and 'From A Window' a US No. 23 and UK No. 10. This is the first of 4 'Shindig!' appearances. During the finale of Jerry Lee Lewis' 'Great Balls Of Fire' he is joined by most of the other performers on the show.

LEON RUSSELL: His performance of 'Hi-Heel Sneakers' works far better instrumentally than it does vocally. Maybe he was distracted by the two short-skirted dancers on top of the piano.

DICK AND DEE DEE: Dick St. John (Richard St. John Gosting, b. 1940 - d. 2003) and Dee Dee Sperling (Mary Spelling). Vocal duo from California. 'Though Shalt Not Steal' was a US No. 13 hit. Semi-regulars on the show, this is the first of 11 'Shindig!' appearances.

CHRIS CROSBY: 'The Glory Of Love' is a track from Chris Crosby's sole album 'Meet Chris Crosby'.

BOBBY SHERMAN: Guitarist Jerry Cole tries to replicate Dave Davies' solo in The Kinks' 'You Really Got Me', and he almost succeeds.

L-R: Leon Russell; The Blossoms; Chris Crosby; Dick and Dee Dee; The Wellingtons; Billy J. Kramer with The Dakotas

Episode 8: 4th November 1964

Gerry and The Pacemakers - How Do You Do It?
The Righteous Brothers - In That Great Getting' Up Mornin'
Glen Campbell - Summer, Winter, Spring, Fall
Ketty Lester - You Can Have Him
Gene Pitney - I'm Gonna Be Strong
The Miracles - You've Really Got A Hold On Me
Glenn Campbell - Ain't That Lovin' You Baby
Ketty Lester - Love Letters
Gerry and The Pacemakers - I Like It
Gerry and The Pacemakers - A Shot Of Rhythm and Blues
The Miracles - Mickey's Monkey

GERRY AND THE PACEMAKERS: Gerry Marsden (Gerard Marsden, b. 1942 - d. 2021 - vocals and guitar), Les Chadwick (John Leslie Chadwick, b. 1943 - d. 2019 - bass), Freddie Marsden (Frederick Marsden, b. 1940 - d. 2006 - drums and backing vocals) and Les Maguire (Leslie Charles Maguire, b. 1941 - piano and backing vocals). Beat Group from Liverpool. 'How Do You Do It?' was a US No. 9 and 'I Like It' a US No. 17, and both songs topped the charts in the UK. This is the first of 6 'Shindig!' appearances. This performance of 'How Do You Do It?' sees the band arrive in a (fake) vintage car, while 'I Like It' features Gerry Marsden in a barber's chair.

GLEN CAMPBELL: Glen Travis Campbell (b. 1936 - d. 2017). Singer and guitarist from Billstown, Arkansas. 'Summer, Winter, Spring, Fall' was his latest single, while 'Ain't That Lovin' You Baby' is a surprisingly good version of the Elvis Presley hit. As well as guesting on the very first Pilot show, he made 21 'Shindig!' appearances.

KETTY LESTER: Revoyda Frierson (b. 1934). Pop and Soul singer from Hope, Arkansas. 1962's 'Love Letters' was a US Pop No. 5, R&B No. 2 and UK No. 4. This is the first of 2 'Shindig!' appearances. 'You Can Have Him' is a gender-reversed version of Roy Hamilton's 'You Can Have Her'.

GENE PITNEY: Gene Francis Alan Pitney (b. 1940 - d. 2006). Pop singer and songwriter from Hartford, Connecticut. 'I'm Gonna Be Strong' was a US No. 9 and UK No. 2. This is the first of 2 'Shindig!' appearances.

THE MIRACLES: Smokey Robinson (William Robinson Jr., b. 1940), Ronnie White (Ronald Anthony White, b. 1939 - d. 1995), Pete Moore (Warren Thomas Moore, b. 1938 - d. 2017), Bobby Rogers (Robert Edward Rogers, b. 1940 - d. 2013) and Marv Tarplin (Marvin Tarplin, b. 1941 - d. 2011 - guitar). Rhythm 'n' Blues and Soul group from Detroit, Michigan. 1962's 'You've Really Got A Hold On Me' was a US Pop No. 8 and R&B No. 1, and the following year's 'Mickey's Monkey' a US Pop No. 8 and R&B No. 3.

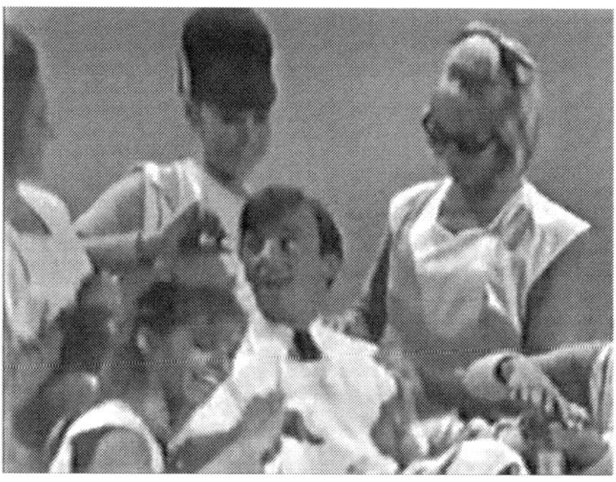

L-R: The Righteous Brothers; Glen Campbell; Gene Pitney; The Miracles; Ketty Lester; Gerry and The Pacemakers

Episode 9: 11th November 1964

Billy J. Kramer with The Dakotas - I Call Your Name
Bobby Sherman - I'm Into Something Good
The Apollas - Swing Down, Sweet Chariot
Hank Williams Jr. - Endless Sleep
Russ Titleman - Things We Said Today
Orriel Smith - Black Is The Color
Billy J. Kramer with The Dakotas - Tennessee Waltz
Jody Miller - I Can't Believe What You Say (For Seeing What You Do)
Bobby Sherman - She's Not There
Willy Nelson - The Girl Can't Help It

BILLY J. KRAMER AND THE DAKOTAS: Recorded and released before The Beatles' own version, Lennon and McCartney's 'I Call Your Name' was the B-side of the 1963 UK chart topper 'Bad To Me'. The most impressive act on this episode, probably the only reason they didn't close it is because they'd already done so just 2 weeks earlier.

THE APOLLAS: Leola Jiles (b. 1942), Ella Jamerson and Dorothy Ramsey. Soul trio from Los Angeles, California, who also recorded as The Lovejoys. 'Swing Down, Sweet Chariot' is a song they never released on record.

HANK WILLIAMS JR.: Randall Hank Williams (b. 1949). Country singer and guitarist from Shreveport, Louisiana. Hank's version of Jody Reynolds' 'Endless Sleep' got to No. 90 in the US Pop charts and No. 46 Country.

RUSS TITLEMAN: (b. 1944). Pop and Soul singer, songwriter and producer from Los Angeles, California. This is the first of 5 'Shindig!' appearances.

ORRIEL SMITH: Opera-trained Folk singer and guitarist from Hollywood, California. The traditional song 'Black Is The Color' is from her 1964 album 'A Voice In The Wind'.

JODY MILLER: While she's no Tina Turner, 'I Can't Believe What You Say (For Seeing What You Do)' is an enjoyably good version of an Ike and Tina Turner song.

BOBBY SHERMAN: In contrast to The Blossoms and Donna Loren, Bobby Sherman's covers were often inferior to the originals. The Zombies' 'She's Not There' is a prime example.

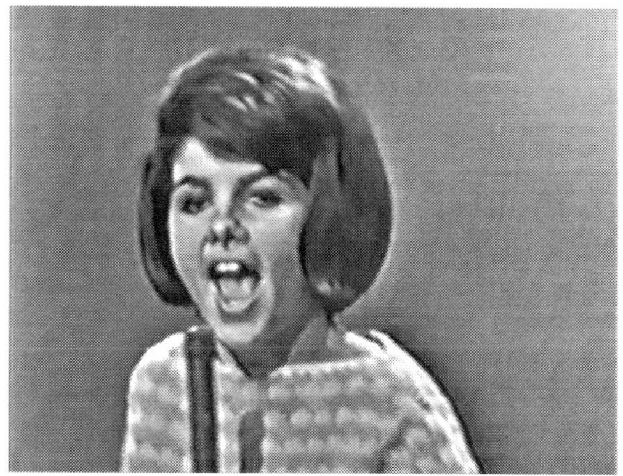

L-R: Billy J. Kramer with The Dakotas; The Apollas; Hank Williams Jr.; Russ Titleman; Orriel Smith; Jody Miller

Episode 10: 18th November 1964 (Part 1 of 2)

Leon Russell - Roll Over Beethoven
Jackie and Gayle - You Should Have Seen The Way He Looked At Me
Bobby DoQui and **Arnold Rollin** - Round About The Mountain
Paul Petersen - My Dad
The Supremes - Baby Love
Donna Loren - African Waltz
Bill Medley - Georgia On My Mind
The Righteous Brothers - Ko Ko Joe
The Supremes - Come See About Me
Paul Petersen - She Can't Find Her Keys
The Righteous Brothers - Little Latin Lupe Lu

LEON RUSSELL: This starts with a snippet of music by Ludwig Van Beethoven before launching into a Jerry Lee Lewis-styled version of the song.

BOBBY DOQUI AND ARNOLD ROLLIN: Folk and Gospel duo from California. Bobby DoQui (b. 1934 - d. 2008) would later become a well known actor under his real name Robert DoQui.

PAUL PETERSEN: Paul William Petersen (b. 1945). Actor and Pop singer from Glendale, California. 1962's 'My Dad' was a US Pop No. 6 and Adult Contemporary No. 2.

THE SUPREMES: Diana Ross (b. 1944), Mary Wilson (b. 1944 - d. 2021) and Florence Ballard (b. 1943 - d. 1976). Soul and pop vocal trio from Detroit, Michigan. 'Baby Love' topped the charts in the US and UK, and 'Come See About Me' was a US No. 1 and UK No. 27. This is the first of 2 'Shindig!' appearances.

THE RIGHTEOUS BROTHERS: 'Ko Ko Joe' was originally released by Don and Dewey, a Rhythm 'n' Blues duo who were a major influence on The Righteous Brothers' uninhibited early recordings.

This is the first of 2 'Shindig!' episodes broadcast on the same day.

L-R: Leon Russell; Jackie and Gayle; Bobby Doqui and Arnold Rollin; Paul Petersen; The Supremes; Donna Loren

Episode 11: 18th November 1964 (Part 2 of 2)

Opening Medley: **Carolyn Daye** - Jump Back / **Bobby Sherman** - I'm Crying / **The Everly Brothers** - Gone, Gone, Gone (End of Medley)

Manfred Mann - Sha La La *

Carolyn Daye - See See Rider

Bessie Griffin and Her Gospel Pearls - Dry Bones

The Wellingtons - Everybody Knows (I Still Love You)

The Blossoms - Needle In A Haystack

Bobby Sherman - Sea Cruise

Bessie Griffin and Her Gospel Pearls - Come On Children

The Everly Brothers - All I Have To Do Is Dream

The Everly Brothers - Bye Bye Love

The Everly Brothers - Rip It Up

MANFRED MANN: 'Sha La La' got to No. 12 in the US and No. 3 in the UK.

CAROLYN DAYE: Pop and Soul singer, probably from California.

BESSIE GRIFFIN AND HER GOSPEL PEARLS: Bessie Griffin (b. 1922 - d. 1989). Gospel vocal group from New Orleans, Louisiana.

THE WELLINGTONS: 'Everybody Knows (I Still Love You)' is an interesting version of the Dave Clark Five hit.

THE BLOSSOMS: Thanks in no small part to Darlene Love's lead vocals, this performance of The Velvelettes' 'Needle In A Haystack' surpasses the original.

THE EVERLY BROTHERS: Their latest single 'Gone, Gone, Gone' was a US No. 31 and UK No. 36, 1959's 'All I Have To Do Is Dream' was a US No. 1 in Pop, C&W and R&B as well as in the UK, their 1957 debut hit 'Bye Bye Love' reached No. 2 Pop, No. 1 C&W, No. 5 R&B and No. 6 in the UK, and 'Rip It Up' was on their first album. Still at the peak of their considerable abilities, The Everly Brothers were never less than memorable on every 'Shindig!' appearance.

This is the second of 2 'Shindig!' episodes broadcast on the same day.

L-R: Manfred Mann; Carolyn Daye; Bessie Griffin and Her Gospel Pearls; The Wellingtons; The Blossoms; The Everly Brothers

Episode 12: 25th November 1964

Opening Medley: **The Righteous Brothers** - She's Not There / **Donna Loren** - Ain't That Lovin' You Baby / **Chad and Jeremy** - Yesterday's Gone / **Matt Monro** - My Kind Of Girl / **Tina Turner** - A Fool In Love / **Neil Sedaka** - Next Door To An Angel (End of Medley)

Chad and Jeremy - If She Was Mine

Donna Loren - Too Many Fish In The Sea

The Righteous Brothers - This Little Girl Of Mine

Neil Sedaka - I Hope He Breaks Your Heart

Matt Monro - Walk Away

Tina Turner - A Fool In Love

Chad and Jeremy - Willow Weep For Me

Neil Sedaka - Calendar Girl

Neil Sedaka - Little Devil

Tina Turner - Ooh Poop A Doo

NEIL SEDAKA: (b. 1939). Singer, pianist and songwriter from Brooklyn, New York. 1962's 'Next Door To An Angel' was a US Pop No. 5, R&B No. 19 and UK No. 29, 'I Hope He Breaks Your Heart' was a US No. 104, 1961's 'Calendar Girl' a US No. 4 and UK No. 8, and the same year's 'Little Devil' a US No. 11. This is the first of 3 'Shindig!' appearances.

CHAD AND JEREMY: Chad Stuart (David Stuart Chadwick, b. 1941 - d. 2020) and Jeremy Clyde (Michael Thomas Jeremy Clyde, b. 1941). Pop and Folk duo from UK. 'Yesterday's Gone' got to No. 21 in the US charts and No. 37 in the UK (their only UK hit), and 'Willow Weep For Me' reached No. 15 in the US. This is the first of 2 'Shindig!' appearances.

DONNA LOREN: An excellent version of The Marvelettes' 'Too Many Fish In The Sea', with Donna looking as good as she sounds.

THE RIGHTEOUS BROTHERS: 'This Little Girl Of Mine' owes more to Ray Charles' original than the perhaps better-known cover by The Everly Brothers.

MATT MONRO: Terence Edward Parsons (b. 1930 - d. 1985). Pop and Easy listening singer from London, UK. 1961's 'My Kind Of Girl' was a UK No. 3 hit, and his recent single 'Walk Away' was a US No. 135 and UK No. 4. A fine singer in the Frank Sinatra mode, he both looks and sounds out of place on this show, particularly when followed by Tina Turner.

TINA TURNER: Anna Mae Bullock (b. 1939). Rhythm 'n' Blues and Soul singer from Brownsville, Tennessee. Ike and Tina Turner's 'A Fool In Love' was a US Pop No. 27 and R&B No. 2 in 1960, and 'Ooh Poop A Doo' was a flop single in 1964. This is the first of 3 'Shindig!' appearances for Tina Turner - all of them without Ike. Her slightly renamed cover of Jessie Hill's 'Ooh Poo Pah Doo' features Neil Sedaka on piano and The Blossoms on backing vocals.

L-R: Chad and Jeremy; Donna Loren; The Righteous Brothers; Neil Sedaka; Matt Monro; Tina Turner

Episode 13: 2nd December 1964

Opening Medley: **Bobby Sherman** - Hot Dog / **Donna Loren** - Just Because / **Freddy Cannon** - Abigail Beecher / **The Chambers Brothers, The Righteous Brothers** and **The Blossoms** - Shout (End of Medley)

Donna Loren - Rock Me In The Cradle Of Love

Bobby Sherman and **Donna Loren** - Casting My Spell

Bobby Vinton - Mr. Lonely

Aretha Franklin - Won't Be Long

The Righteous Brothers - Baby What You Want Me To Do

Freddy Cannon - Too Much Monkey Business

Aretha Franklin - Runnin' Out Of Fools

Bobby Sherman - Farmer John

Bobby Vinton - Roses Are Red (My Love)

The Chambers Brothers - Rough and Rocky Road (I Feel Like Crying All The Time)

FREDDY CANNON: Frederick Anthony Picariello Jr. (b. 1936). Rock 'n' Roll and Pop singer from Revere, Massachusetts. 'Abigail Beecher' was a No. 16 US hit, while his single of Chuck Berry's 'Too Much Monkey Business' failed to chart.

DONNA LOREN: Her fine version of 'Rock Me In The Cradle Of Love' was originally by Dee Dee Sharp, and her duet with Bobby Sherman 'Casting My Spell' is a Johnny Otis song.

BOBBY VINTON: Stanley Robert Vinton Jr. (b. 1935). Pop singer from Canonsburg, Pennsylvania. His latest single, 'Mr. Lonely' topped the US charts, as did 1962's 'Roses Are Red (My Love)' which also got to No. 15 in the UK.

ARETHA FRANKLIN: Aretha Louise Franklin (b. 1942 - d. 2018). Soul and Pop singer and pianist from Detroit, Michigan. 1960's 'Won't Be Long' was a US Pop No. 76 and R&B No. 7, and the recent single 'Runnin' Out Of Fools' got to No. 57 in Pop and No. 30 in R&B. This is the first of 4 'Shindig!' appearances.

THE CHAMBERS BROTHERS: 'Rough and Rocky Road (I Feel Like Crying All The Time)' is a noisy but inspirational Gospel finale.

L-R: Bobby Sherman and Donna Loren; Bobby Vinton; Aretha Franklin; The Righteous Brothers; Freddy Cannon; The Chambers Brothers

Episode 14: 9th December 1964

Tommy Quickly - The Dog
Manfred Mann - Do Wah Diddy Diddy
Kelly Garrett - Mellow Fellow
Chubby Checker - She Wants T'Swim
The Dixie Cups - Chapel Of Love
The Dixie Cups - You Should Have Seen The Way He Looked At Me
The Righteous Brothers - Fannie Mae
Willy Nelson - Hand Jive
Tommy Quickly - The Wild Side Of Life
Chubby Checker - Lovely Lovely (Loverly Loverly)
Manfred Mann - Sha La La

TOMMY QUICKLY: 'The Wild Side Of Life' was Tommy Quickly's sole UK hit, peaking at No. 33, though he sounds more at home with the tough Rhythm 'n' Blues of Rufus Thomas' 'The Dog'.

MANFRED MANN: 'Do Wah Diddy Diddy' and 'Sha La La' are both 2nd 'Shindig!' performances of their big hits, though this time they're actually live in the 'Shindig!' studio rather than pre-taped in London.

KELLY GARRETT: Ellen Boulton (b. 1944 - d. 2013). Singer and actress from Chester, Pennsylvania. This is the first of 4 'Shindig!' appearances, and she proves herself a more than capable vocalist even when tackling a song originally done by Etta James.

CHUBBY CHECKER: Ernest Evans (b. 1941). Rock 'n' Roll and Pop singer from Philadelphia, Pennsylvania. 'She Wants T'Swim' was a No. 50 US hit and 'Lovely, Lovely (Loverly, Loverly)' peaked at No. 70. An underrated performer, the material here isn't his best, and it probably would've been wiser if he'd dug out one of his old hits.

THE DIXIE CUPS: Barbara Ann Hawkins (b. 1943), Rosa Lee Hawkins (b. 1944) and Joan Marie Johnson (b. 1945 - d. 2016). Girl group from New Orleans, Louisiana. 'Chapel Of Love' topped the charts in the US and got to No. 22 in the UK, while 'You Should Have Seen The Way He Looked At Me' peaked at US No. 39. This is the first of 2 'Shindig!' appearances, marred only slightly by 'Chapel Of Love' being a very short version.

THE RIGHTEOUS BROTHERS - Originally by Buster Brown, 'Fannie Mae' was also covered by The Rolling Stones for a BBC radio performance.

L-R: Manfred Mann; Kelly Garrett; Chubby Checker; The Dixie Cups; Willy Nelson; Tommy Quickly

Episode 15: 16th December 1964

The Dave Clark Five - Medley: Zip-A-Dee-Doo-Dah / Can't You See That She's Mine
Mickey Rooney Jr. - I Feel Fine
The Newbeats - Everything's Alright
Adam Faith - Boom Boom
Kelly Garrett - Wild One
Bobby Sherman - She's A Woman
The Blossoms - Going Out Of My Head
Adam Faith - It's Alright
The Dave Clark Five - Everybody Knows (I Still Love You)
The Dave Clark Five - Any Way You Want It
The Isley Brothers - Shout

THE DAVE CLARK FIVE: Dave Clark (b. 1939 - drums and occasional lead vocals), Mike Smith (Michael George Smith, b. 1943 - d. 2008 - lead vocals and keyboards), Lenny Davidson (Leonard Arthur Davidson, b. 1944 - guitar and occasional lead vocals), Rick Huxley (b. 1940 - d. 2013 - bass) and Denis Payton (Denis Archibald West Payton, b. 1943 - d. 2006 - saxophone, harmonica, guitar and occasional lead vocals). Beat group from Tottenham, London, UK. 'Can't You See That She's Mine' got to No. 4 in the US and No. 10 in the UK, 'Everybody Knows (I Still Love You)' was a US No. 15 and UK No. 37, and 'Any Way You Want It' a US No. 14 and UK No. 25. This is the first of 6 'Shindig!' appearances.

MICKEY ROONEY Jr.: Ninnian Joseph Yule III (b. 1945). Actor and singer from Birmingham, Alabama. This is the first of 2 'Shindig!' appearances. His version of The Beatles' 'I Feel Fine' is acceptable enough.

THE NEWBEATS: Not to be confused with the song by UK group The Mojos, 'Everything Alright' was a No. 16 US hit.

ADAM FAITH: Another performance of 'It's Alright', his biggest US hit. For someone known in the UK for lightweight pop, he handles John Lee Hooker's 'Boom Boom' with surprising ease.

THE BLOSSOMS: Their cover of Little Anthony and The Imperials' 'Going Out Of My Head' features Fanita James singing lead rather than the usual Darlene Love.

THE ISLEY BROTHERS: Ronald Isley (b. 1941), Rudolph Isley (Rudolph Bernard Isley, b. 1939) and O'Kelly Isley (O'Kelly Isley Jr., b. 1937 - d. 1986). Rhythm 'n' Blues and Soul group from Cincinnati, Ohio. Their first hit in 1959, 'Shout' got to No. 47 in the US charts, though it is better known by Lulu in the UK. They never sounded more frantic than on this inspired live version.

L-R: The Dave Clark Five; Mickey Rooney Jr.; The Newbeats; Adam Faith; The Blossoms; The Isley Brothers

Episode 16: 23rd December 1964

The Beach Boys - Dance, Dance, Dance
Bobby Sherman and **Donna Loren** - Keep Searchin' (We'll Follow The Show)
The Righteous Brothers - The Jerk
Marvin Gaye - How Sweet It Is (To Be Loved By You)
Adam Faith - Watch Your Step
Bobby Sherman - Sleigh Ride
Adam Faith - Santa Claus Is Back In Town
Donna Loren - Santa Claus Is Coming To Town
The Beach Boys - Little Saint Nick
The Beach Boys - Monster Mash
The Beach Boys - Papa Oom Mow Mow
The Beach Boys - Johnny B. Goode
Marvin Gaye - Hitch Hike
The Beach Boys - We Three Kings

NOTE: The available master has been edited, so running order may not be 100% correct!

THE BEACH BOYS: Mike Love (Michael Edward Love, b. 1941 - vocals and occasional saxophone), Carl Wilson (Carl Dean Wilson, b. 1946 - d. 1998 - vocals and guitar), Al Jardine (Alan Charles Jardine, b. 1942 - vocals and guitar), Brian Wilson (Brian Douglas Wilson, b. 1942 - vocals and bass) and Dennis Wilson (Dennis Carl Wilson, b. 1944 - d. 1983 - vocals and drums). Surf and Pop band from Hawthorne, California. 'Dance, Dance, Dance' got to No. 8 in the US charts and No. 24 in the UK, and 'Little Saint Nick' peaked at US No. 47. This is the first of 2 'Shindig!' appearances. The Beach Boys were always great fun live, even if Mike Love's dancing is a bit of an embarrassment.

ADAM FAITH: Once again he proves more than capable of performing tougher material like Bobby Parker's 'Watch Your Step' and Elvis Presley's 'Santa Claus Is Back In Town'.

DONNA LOREN: Her strong version of 'Santa Claus Is Coming To Town' is a show highlight.

MARVIN GAYE: Marvin Pentz Gay Jr. (b. 1939 - d. 1984). Soul singer from Washington, D.C.. 'How Sweet It Is (To Be Loved By You)' was a US Pop No. 6, R&B No. 3 and UK No. 49, and 1962's 'Hitch Hike' got to US Pop No. 30 and R&B No. 12. This is the first of 2 'Shindig!' appearances. On both songs he is ably backed by The Blossoms.

L-R: Bobby Sherman and Donna Loren; The Righteous Brothers; Marvin Gaye; Adam Faith, Donna Loren; The Beach Boys

Episode 17: 30th December 1964

Opening Medley: **Donna Loren**, **The Wellingtons** and **The Blossoms** - At The Hop / **Willy Nelson** and **The Blossoms** - Long Tall Sally / **The Wellingtons** - At The Hop (Reprise) / **Jerry Lee Lewis** - Jenny Jenny (End of Medley)

Mary Wells - My Guy

Willy Nelson, **The Wellingtons** and **The Blossoms** - Don't Let Go

The Gauchos - California Sun

Vic Dana - Down By The Riverside

Donna Loren - Ten Good Reasons

Jerry Lee Lewis - Mean Woman Blues

Mary Wells - Use Your Head

Bobby Rydell - I Just Can't Say Goodbye

Bobby Rydell - Swingin' School

Jerry Lee Lewis - Whole Lotta Shakin' Going On

JERRY LEE LEWIS: (b. 1935). Rock 'n' Roll and Country singer and pianist from Ferriday, Louisiana. 'Jenny Jenny' and 'Mean Woman Blues' were both included on his latest album 'The Greatest Live Show On Earth' with the latter also on a 1957 EP, and 1957's 'Whole Lotta Shakin' Going On' got to No. 3 in US Pop, No. 1 C&W, No. 1 R&B and No. 8 in the UK. This is the first of 5 'Shindig!' appearances, every one of them featuring him at his very wildest. During 'Whole Lotta Shakin' Going On' guitarist Jerry Cole climbs on top of the piano, to be quickly joined by Jerry Lee Lewis who clearly didn't wasn't about to be upstaged.

MARY WELLS: Mary Esther Wells (b. 1943 - d. 1992). Rhythm 'n' Blues and Soul singer from Detroit, Michigan. 'My Guy' was a US No. 1 and UK No. 5, and her latest record 'Use Your Head' a US No. 34. Also performed here is 'When I'm Gone', a record that was cancelled as a single release due to Mary being in dispute with Motown and leaving the company; it was subsequently a US No. 13 hit for Brenda Holloway. This is the first of 2 'Shindig!' appearances.

THE GAUCHOS: Sometimes billed as Jim Doval and The Gauchos, this Latin-American band made 6 'Shindig!' appearances.

VIC DANA: Samuel Mendola (b. 1940). Pop singer from Buffalo, New York. The first of 2 'Shindig!' appearances, his swing arrangement of the old spiritual 'Down By The Riverside' is dreadful.

BOBBY RYDELL: Robert Louis Ridarelli (b. 1942). Rock 'n' Roll and Pop singer from Philadelphia, Pennsylvania. His latest single, 'I Just Can't Say Good Bye' was a US No. 94 hit, and 1960's 'Swingin' School' got to No. 5 in the US and No. 44 in the UK.

L-R: Mary Wells; The Gauchos; Vic Dana; Donna Loren; Bobby Rydell; Jerry Lee Lewis

Episode 18: 6th January 1965

Opening Medley: **Jackie and Gayle** and **The Righteous Brothers** - Let The Good Times Roll / **Donna Loren** and **The Blossoms** - Too Many Fish In The Sea / **Bobby Sherman** - Hound Dog (End of Medley)

Adam Faith - Don't You Dig This Kind Of Beat

The Blossoms - Swing Down Sweet Chariot

Sandie Shaw - (There's) Always Something There To Remind Me *

Jackie and Gayle - Why Can't My Teacher Look Like Mr Novak?

Donna Loren - 90 Day Guarantee

The Righteous Brothers - Charlie Brown

Bobby Sherman - High School Confidential

Sal Mineo - The Girl Across The Way

Sal Mineo - Save The Last Dance For Me

The Righteous Brothers - In That Great Gettin' Up Mornin'

SANDIE SHAW: Sandie's UK No. 1, this is a different performance to the one in Episode 4.

JACKIE AND GAYLE: The so-good-it's-bad 'Why Can't My Teacher Look Like Mr Novak?' was released as Jackie and Gayle's first single, and is enhanced further here by a cameo from Jack Good.

THE RIGHTEOUS BROTHERS: The Coasters' 'Charlie Brown' is performed as part of a short sketch featuring the duo working behind a counter in an ice-cream store.

SAL MINEO: Salvatore Mineo Jr. (b. 1939 - d. 1976). Actor and singer from New York City. 'The Girl Across The Way' and 'Save The Last Dance For Me' were both released as singles that failed to chart, possibly because he was a far better actor than singer.

L-R: Adam Faith; The Blossoms; Sandie Shaw; Jackie and Gayle, The Righteous Brothers; Sal Mineo

Episode 19: 13th January 1965

Dick and Dee Dee - Thou Shalt Not Steal
Herman's Hermits - I'm Into Something Good *
Paul Peterson - Little Dreamer
Johnny Cash - Amen (with The Statler Brothers and The Blossoms)
The Detergents - Leader Of The Laundromat
Dick and Dee Dee - Be My Baby
The Righteous Brothers - You've Lost That Lovin' Feelin'
The Paris Sisters - My Buddy
Johnny Cash - Orange Blossom Special
Paul Peterson - I'm In Love Again

DICK AND DEE DEE: Another performance of their US No. 13 hit from this under-appreciated pop duo.

HERMAN'S HERMITS: Peter Noone (Peter Blair Denis Bernard Noone, b. 1947 - vocals), Derek Leckenby (b. 1943 - d. 1994 - guitar), Keith Hopwood (b. 1946 - guitar and vocals), Karl Green (Karl Anthony Green, b. 1947 - bass and vocals) and Barry Whitwam (Jan Barry Whitwam, b. 1946 - drums). Beat Group from Manchester, UK. 'I'm Into Something Good' got to No. 13 in the US and topped the charts in the UK. This is the first of 2 'Shindig!' appearances.

THE DETERGENTS: Ron Dante (Carmine Granito, b. 1945), Danny Jordan (Gerard Jerry Florio) and Tommy Wymn. Vocal group from New York City. A lame spoof of the Shangri-Las' 'Leader of the Pack', 'Leader Of The Laundromat' got to No. 19 in the US charts.

THE RIGHTEOUS BROTHERS: Their biggest hit and a dramatic change of style from the Rhythm 'n' Blues of old, 'You've Lost That Lovin' Feelin'' topped the charts in both the USA and UK.

THE PARIS SISTERS: Priscilla Paris (b. 1941 - d. 2004), Albeth Paris (Albeth Carole Paris, b. 1935 - d. 2014) and Sherrell Paris. Pop vocal trio from San Francisco, California.

JOHNNY CASH: A 1965 single, 'Orange Blossom Special' reached No. 80 in the US Pop charts and No. 3 in C&W, this animated live performance features Johnny Cash dressed as a railway bum.

PAUL PETERSON: His performance of 'I'm In Love Again' shows that Paul Peterson is no Fats Domino (Fats himself was one of the few big-selling '50s/early '60s Rock 'n' Roll stars who never appeared on 'Shindig!').

L-R: Herman's Hermits; Paul Peterson; The Detergents; The Righteous Brothers; The Paris Sisters; Johnny Cash

Episode 20: 20th January 1965

Opening Medley: **Bobby Sherman** - I Can't Stop / **Jackie and Gayle** - Give Him A Great Big Kiss / **The Walker Brothers** - I'm A Loser / **Donna Loren** - Rock 'N' Roll Music / **Glen Campbell** - Mean Woman Blues (End of Medley)
The Kinks - You Really Got Me *
Jackie and Gayle - Yakety Yak
Glen Campbell - Crying
Gerry and The Pacemakers - Dizzy Miss Lizzy
Petula Clark - Downtown
The Walker Brothers - Promised Land
Bobby Sherman - That Is Rock 'N' Roll
The Dave Clark Five - Because + Glad All Over
Bobby Vee - Cross My Heart
Roosevelt 'Rosey' Grier - I Who Have Nothing
The Fearsome Foursome - Since You're Gone
The Kinks - All Day and All Of The Night *
Donna Loren - Ten Good Reasons
Bobby Vee - Early In The Morning
The Walker Brothers - Pretty Girls Everywhere
Donna Loren - Boys
Bobby Sherman - Girls! Girls! Girls!
Gerry and The Pacemakers - Don't Let The Sun Catch You Crying
The Rolling Stones - Heart Of Stone *
Glen Campbell - Dream Baby

THE KINKS: Ray Davies (Raymond Douglas Davies, b. 1944 - vocals, guitar, harmonica and keyboards), Dave Davies (David Russell Gordon Davies, b. 1947 - guitar and vocals), Pete Quaife (Peter Alexander Greenlaw Kinnes, b. 1943 - d. 2010 - bass) and Mick Avory (Michael Charles Avory, b. 1944 - drums). Rhythm 'n' Blues and Pop band from Muswell Hill, London, UK. 'You Really Got Me' was a US No. 7 and UK. 1, and 'All Day and All Of The Night' a US No. 7 and UK No. 2. Taped in London on 17th December 1964, this was the first of 6 'Shindig!' appearances.

GLEN CAMPBELL: Glen Campbell sounds uncannily like Roy Orbison on 'Crying' and 'Dream Baby'.

PETULA CLARK: Sally Olwen Clark (b. 1932). Pop singer from Ewell, Surrey, UK. 'Downtown' topped the US charts and peaked at No. 2 in the UK. This was the first of 2 'Shindig!' appearances.

BOBBY SHERMAN: Both 'That Is Rock 'N' Roll' and 'Girls! Girls! Girls!' were originally recorded by The Coasters.

THE DAVE CLARK FIVE: 'Because' was a No. 3 US hit but just a B-side in the UK, and 'Glad All Over' reached No. 6 in the US and topped the charts in the UK.

BOBBY VEE: Robert Thomas Velline (b. 1943 - d. 2016). Rock 'n' Roll and Pop singer from Fargo, North Dakota. 'Cross My Heart' was a minor US hit at No. 99, and 'Early In The Morning' is from the 1963 'I Remember Buddy Holly' album.

THE FEARSOME FOURSOME: Roosevelt 'Rosey' Grier (b. 1932), Merlin Olsen (b. 1940 - d. 2010), Lamar Lundy and David 'Deacon' Jones. American Football players and occasional singers from Los Angeles. Roosevelt 'Rosey' Grier also made 2 solo 'Shindig!' appearances, and was a member of The New Yorkers who would appear in Episode 25.

THE WALKER BROTHERS: 'Pretty Girls Everywhere' was The Walker Brothers' first, non-charting, single.

GERRY AND THE PACEMAKERS: 'Don't Let The Sun Catch You Crying' got to No. 4 in the US and No. 6 in the UK.

THE ROLLING STONES: Mick Jagger (Michael Philip Jagger, b. 1943 - vocals and harmonica), Keith Richards (b. 1943 - guitar and vocals), Brian Jones (Lewis Brian Hopkin Jones, b. 1942 - d. 1969 - guitar and harmonica), Bill Wyman (William George Perks, b. 1936 - bass) and Charlie Watts (Charles Robert Watts, b. 1941 - drums). Rhythm 'n' Blues and Pop group from London, UK. 'Heart Of Stone' was a US No. 19 hit, as well as a track on the US 'The Rolling Stones, Now!' and the UK 'Out Of Our Heads' albums. This performance was taped in London on 12th December 1964.

L-R: Petula Clark; The Rolling Stones; The Kinks; The Dave Clark Five; Gerry and The Pacemakers; Bobby Vee

Episode 21: 27th January 1965

Opening Medley: **Glen Campbell** - Dixieland Rock / **Little Anthony and The Imperials** - Way Down Yonder In New Orleans / **Bobby Sherman** - New Orleans / **The Serendipity Singers** - Battle Of New Orleans / **The Blossoms** and **Bill Medley** - Muskrat Ramble / **Little Anthony and The Imperials** - Dixieland Rock (End of Medley)
Susan Barrett - Jim Dandy
Bobby Sherman - You Can't Sit Down
Bobby Hatfield - Good Golly Miss Molly
The Righteous Brothers - What'd I Say
Ray Peterson - Unchained Melody
Freddie and The Dreamers - You Were Made For Me*
Duane Eddy - Roughneck
Aretha Franklin - Can't You Just See Me
Glen Campbell - Kentucky Means Paradise
The Gloria Tracy Trio - Love For Sale
The Zombies - Tell Her No *
The Serendipity Singers - Rider
Glen Campbell - Cumberland Gap
Little Anthony and The Imperials - Hurt So Bad
Bobby Sherman - Splish Splash
Aretha Franklin - Rock-A-Bye Your Baby With A Dixie Melody
Duane Eddy - Rebel-'Rouser
Susan Barrett - Mr. Lee
John Andrea - Take Her
The Serendipity Singers - Little Brown Jug
The Righteous Brothers - Look At Me
Little Anthony and The Imperials - Medley: Twist and Shout / Shout

SUSAN BARRETT: Susan Marie Barrett (b. 1934 - d. 2001). Soul and pop singer from Nashville, Tennessee.

RAY PETERSON: Ray T. Peterson (b. 1935 - d. 2005). Pop and Country singer from Denton, Texas. This is the first of 5 'Shindig!' appearances.

FREDDIE AND THE DREAMERS: Freddie Garrity (Frederick Garrity, b. 1936 - d. 2006 - vocals), Roy Crewdson (b. 1941 - guitar), Derek Quinn (b. 1942 - d. 2020 - guitar and harmonica), Pete Birrell (Peter Birrell, b. 1941 - bass and vocals) and Bernie Dwyer (b. 1940 - d. 2002 - drums). Beat Group from Manchester, UK. 'You Were Made For Me' got to No. 3 in the UK charts in 1963, and No. 21 in the US in 1965. This was the first of 4 'Shindig!' appearances.

DUANE EDDY: (b. 1938). Rock 'n' Roll and Pop guitarist from Coolidge, Arizona. 'Roughneck' was the B-side of his current single 'Moon Shot', and 1958's 'Rebel-'Rouser' was a US No. 6 and UK No. 19.

ARETHA FRANKLIN: Her latest single, 'Can't You Just See Me' was a US No. 96, and 1961's 'Rock-A-Bye Your Baby With A Dixie Melody' got to No. 37.

THE GLORIA TRACY TRIO: Jazz and Pop Harp player and backing duo. They sound very out of place here.

THE ZOMBIES: Colin Blunstone (Colin Edward Michael Blunstone, b. 1945 - vocals), Rod Argent (Rodney Terence Argent, b. 1945 - keyboards and vocals), Paul Atkinson (Paul Ashley Warren Atkinson, b. 1946 - d. 2004 - guitar), Chris White (Christopher Taylor White, b. 1943 - bass) and Hugh Grundy (Hugh Birch Grundy, b. 1945 - drums). Beat group from St. Albans, Hertfordshire, UK. 'Tell Her No' got to No. 6 in the US and No. 42 in the UK. This is the first of 3 'Shindig!' appearances.

THE SERENDIPITY SINGERS: Folk and Pop vocal group from Greenwich Village, New York.

LITTLE ANTHONY AND THE IMPERIALS: Little Anthony (Jerome Anthony Gourdine), Ernest Wright, Clarence Collins (Clarence Eugene Collins) and Sam Strain. Rhythm 'n' Blues and Soul group from Brooklyn, New York. 'Hurt So Bad' was a US Pop No. 10 and R&B No. 3. This is the first of 2 'Shindig!' appearances.

L-R: Freddie and The Dreamers; Duane Eddy; Aretha Franklin; The Zombies; Susan Barrett; Little Anthony and The Imperials

Episode 22: 3rd February 1965

Opening Medley: **Donna Loren** - Keep A Knockin' / **The Hondells** - Little Honda / **The Blossoms** - (I Do The) Shimmy Shimmy / **Glen Campbell** - Shake, Rattle and Roll (End of Medley)
Donna Loren - Personality
Bobby Sherman - Rockin' Pneumonia and The Boogie Woogie Flu
The Hondells - Hot Rod High
Russ Titleman (with **Jackie and Gayle** and 5 **Shindig Dancers**) - Seven Little Girls Sitting In The Backseat
The Clara Ward Singers - Didn't It Rain?
The Kingsmen - Little Latin Lupe Lu
Jackie and Gayle - Love Potion No. 9
George and Teddy and The Condors - Sticks and Stones
Donna Loren - The Wedding
Leon Russell - Jambalaya (On The Bayou)
Glen Campbell - Truck Drivin' Man
Gale Garnett - Lovin' Place
Bobby Sherman - You Better Know It
Peter and Gordon - I Go To Pieces + Love Me Baby
The Hondells - You're Gonna Ride With Me
The Shindig Dancers - Bad Motorcycle
John Andrea - Are You Sincere?
George and Teddy and The Condors - Rockin' Robin
The Kingsmen - The Jolly Green Giant
Donna Loren, **Bobby Sherman**, **Gale Garnett** and **Glen Campbell** - Shake A Hand
Donna Loren, **Bobby Sherman**, **Glen Campbell** and **Jackie and Gayle** - Who Do You Love?
Jackie and Gayle - Turn Around
The Clara Ward Singers - The Old Landmark

BOBBY SHERMAN: 'Rockin' Pneumonia and The Boogie Woogie Flu' features Bobby playing rudimentary drums.

THE CLARA WARD SINGERS: Clara Mae Ward (b. 1924 - d. 1973). Gospel vocal group from Philadelphia, Pennsylvania. 'Didn't It Rain' was a 1965 single for the group. Great as the performance is, it is Clara Ward's hair that really steals the show.

THE KINGSMEN: Lynn Easton (Lynn William Easton - vocals), Mike Mitchell (b. 1944 - d. 2021 - vocals and guitar), Norm Sundholm (bass), Barry Curtis (Curt Bartholomew - keyboards) and Dick Peterson (drums). 'Little Latin Lupe Lu' was a US No. 46, and 'The Jolly Green Giant' a US No. 4. This is the first of 3 'Shindig!' appearances.

GEORGE AND TEDDY AND THE CONDORS: Teddy Brown and George Hamilton. Rhythm 'n' Blues duo and band.

DONNA LOREN: 'The Wedding' was a big UK and US hit for Julie Rogers, and Donna Loren sings it just as good.

LEON RUSSELL: On 'Jambalaya (On The Bayou)' he both looks and sounds like Jerry Lee Lewis' cousin Mickey Gilley.

GLEN CAMPBELL: 'Truck Drivin' Man' was a 1965 hit for Buck Owens.

GALE GARNETT: 'Lovin' Place' got to No. 54 in the US charts.

PETER AND GORDON: Peter Asher (b. 1944) and Gordon Waller (Gordon Trueman Riviere Waller, b. 1945 - d. 2009). Pop duo from the UK. 'I Go To Pieces' was a US No. 9, and 'Love Me Baby' was the B-side. This is the first of 3 'Shindig!' appearances.

JOHN ANDREA: John D'Andrea. Pop singer from New Jersey. He appeared on the show 9 times.

L-R: John Andrea; Glen Campbell; Jackie and Gayle; The Kingsmen; Peter and Gordon, The Clara Ward Singers

Episode 23: 10th February 1965

Willy Nelson, **Pat and Lolly Vegas**, **The Coasters**, **The Ventures**, **Bobby Sherman** and **Donna Loren**, **The Temptations**, **The Eligibles** and **Bobby Hatfield** - It's Alright
Del Shannon - Stranger In Town
The Coasters - Along Came Jones
The Ventures - Diamond Head
Bobby Hatfield - Joy, Joy, Joy (Down In My Heart) + My Prayer
Jewel Akens - The Birds and The Bees
Pat and Lolly Vegas - La Bamba
John Andrea - Lemon Tree
The Eligibles - Zing! Went The Strings Of My Heart
Jean King (of **The Blossoms**) - Somewhere
Donna Loren - The Boy From New York City
The Ventures - Caravan
The Coasters - What Is The Secret Of Your Success?
The Temptations - My Girl
Pat and Lolly Vegas - Write Me Baby Please
Del Shannon - Do You Wanna Dance
Bobby Sherman - It Hurts Me
Marianne Faithfull - As Tears Go By *
Willy Nelson - I'm In Love With The Dancing Girl Working At the Metropole
Jerry Mason - Mala
The Coasters - Searchin'
Del Shannon - Keep Searchin' (We'll Follow The Sun)
John Andrea - Take Her
Bobby Hatfield - Shake
The Temptations - When The Saints Go Marching In

JEWEL AKENS: Jewel Eugene Akens (b. 1933 - d. 2013). Soul and Pop singer from Houston, Texas. The first of 2 appearances on the show, 'The Birds and The Bees' got to No. 3 in the Pop charts and No. 21 in R&B.

THE COASTERS: Carl Gardner (Carl Edward Gardner, b. 1928 - d. 2011), Billy Guy (Frank Phillips, b. 1936 - d. 2002), Earl 'Speedo' Carroll (Earl Carroll - b. 1937 - d. 2012) and Will 'Dub' Jones (b. 1928 - d. 2000). Rhythm 'n' Blues and Rock 'n' Roll vocal group from Los Angeles, California. A 1959 single, 'Along Came Jones' got to No. 9 in the US Pop charts and No. 14 R&B, 'What Is The Secret Of Your Success?' was a 1957 B-side, and the same year's 'Searchin'' got to No. 3 in the US Pop charts, No. 1 in R&B and 30 in the UK. 'What Is The Secret Of Your Success?' is a show highlight.

MARIANNE FAITHFULL: Marianne Evelyn Gabriel Faithfull (b. 1946). Pop and Folk singer from London, UK. 'As Tears Go By' reached No. 22 in the US and No. 9 in the UK. This is the first of 8 'Shindig!' appearances.

JERRY MASON: (b. 1942). Rock 'n' Roll and Pop singer and guitarist from Pittsburgh, Pennsylvania. This is the first of 4 'Shindig!' appearances.

WILLY NELSON: 'I'm In Love With The Dancing Girl Working At the Metropole' was his current single.

DEL SHANNON: Charles Weedon Westover (b. 1934 - d. 1990). Rock 'n' Roll and Pop singer and guitarist from Grand Rapids, Michigan. 'Stranger In Town' was a US No. 30 and UK No. 40 hit, 'Do You Wanna Dance?' a US No. 43, and 'Keep Searchin'' (We'll Follow The Sun)' reached No. 9 in the US and No. 3 in the UK.

THE TEMPTATIONS: David Ruffin (Davis Eli Ruffin, b. 1941 - d. 1991), Eddie Kendricks (Edward James Kendrick, b. 1939 - d. 1992), Paul Williams (b. 1939 - d. 1973), Melvin Franklin (David Melvin English, b. 1942 - d. 1995) and Otis Williams (Otis Miles Jr., b. 1941). Rhythm 'n' Blues and Soul group from Detroit, Michigan. 'My Girl' topped the US Pop and R&B charts, and got to No. 43 in the UK. This live performance is another show highlight.

THE VENTURES: Nokie Edwards (Nole Edwards, b. 1935 - d. 2018 - guitar), Don Wilson (Donald Lee Wilson, b. 1933 - guitar), Bob Bogle (Robert Lenard Bogle, b. 1934 - d. 2009 - bass) and Mel Taylor (b. 1933 - d. 1996 - drums). Mainly instrumental Rock 'n' Roll group from Tacoma, Washington. 'Diamond Head' got to No. 70 in the US charts.

L-R: Jewel Akens; The Coasters; Marianne Faithfull; Del Shannon; The Temptations; The Ventures

Episode 24: 17th February 1965

Opening Medley: **Steve Alaimo** - Jailhouse Rock / **Dee Dee Sharp** - Ride! / **Sonny and Cher** - Can't Buy Me Love / **The Blossoms** - The Name Game / **Jerry Lee Lewis** - Breathless (End of Medley)
Glen Campbell - Oh Boy
Linda Gail Lewis - Let's Jump The Broomstick
Sonny and Cher - Rip It Up
Bobby Sherman - Hey Little Girl
Jerry Cole and **Russ Titleman** - Not Fade Away
Dee Dee Sharp - Let The Sunshine In
The Echoes - Shout
Glen Campbell - Tomorrow Never Comes
Peter and Gordon - A World Without Love
Linda Gail Lewis - Thanks A Lot
Jerry Lee Lewis - Long Tall Sally
The Moody Blues - Go Now *
Sandie Shaw - Girl Don't Come *
The Echoes - Hippy Hippy Shake
Steve Alaimo - Real Live Girl
Herman's Hermits - Can't You Hear My Heart Beat *
Peter and Gordon - Land Of Oden
Vic Dana - Red Roses For A Blue Lady
Sonny and Cher - Baby Don't Go
Jerry Lee Lewis - Baby, Hold Me Close
Dee Dee Sharp - Rock Me In The Cradle Of Love
Linda Gail Lewis - (I'm The Girl) On Wolverton Mountain
Bobby Sherman - It Hurts Me + He's Got The Whole World In His Hands
Jerry Lee Lewis - Great Balls Of Fire

JERRY LEE LEWIS: 1958's 'Breathless' was a US Pop No. 7, C&W No. 4, R&B No. 3 and UK No. 8, the new 'Baby, Hold Me Close' peaked at US No. 129, and 1957's 'Great Balls of Fire' a US Pop No. 2, C&W No. 1, R&B No. 1 and UK No. 1.

LINDA GAIL LEWIS: (b. 1947). Pop and Country singer from Ferriday, Louisiana. The first of 2 'Shindig!' performances.

THE ECHOES: Pop and Rhythm 'n' Blues band from Hong Kong.

GLEN CAMPBELL: His latest single, 'Tomorrow Never Comes' was a No. 118 US hit.

PETER AND GORDON: Lennon-McCartney's 'A World Without Love' topped the charts in both the US and the UK.

THE MOODY BLUES: Denny Laine (Brian Frederick Hines, b. 1944 - vocals and guitar), Clint Warwick (Albert Eccles, b. 1940 - d. 2004 - bass and vocals), Ray Thomas (Raymond Thomas, b. 1941 - d. 2018 - vocals, percussion and harmonica), Graeme Edge (Graeme Charles Edge, b. 1941 - drums) and Mike Pinder (Michael Thomas Pinder, b. 1941 - keyboards and vocals). Rhythm 'n' Blues and Beat group from Birmingham, UK. 'Go Now' was a US No. 10 and UK No. 1. This is the first of 4 'Shindig!' performances.

SANDIE SHAW: Her biggest US hit at No. 42, 'Girl Don't Come' also got to No. 3 in the UK.

STEVE ALAIMO: Charles Stephen Alaimo (b. 1939). Pop singer from New York. 'Real Live Girl' was his latest single.

HERMAN'S HERMITS: Not released as a single in the UK, 'Can't You Hear My Heart Beat' was a US No. 2 hit.

VIC DANA: 'Red Roses For A Blue Lady' got to No. 10 in the US charts.

SONNY AND CHER: Sonny (Salvatore Phillip Bono, b. 1935 - d. 1998) and Cher (Cherilyn Sarkisian, b. 1946). Pop and Folk-Rock duo from Los Angeles, California. 'Baby Don't Go' was a US No. 8 and UK No. 11. This is the first of 6 'Shindig!' appearances.

DEE DEE SHARP: Dione LaRue (b. 1945). Soul singer from Philadelphia, Pennsylvania. 1962's 'Ride!' was a US No. 5 and UK No. 7 hit, and 1963's 'Rock Me In The Cradle Of Love' was a US No. 43. This is the first of 2 'Shindig!' appearances.

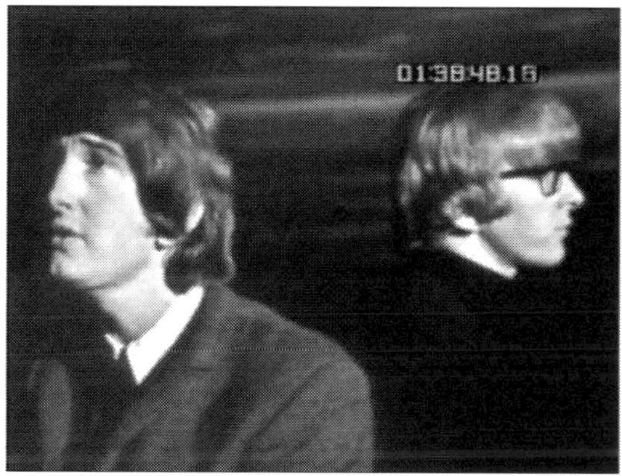

L-R: Jerry Lee Lewis; Sonny and Cher; Dee Dee Sharp; The Moody Blues; Peter and Gordon; Linda Gail Lewis

Episode 25: 24th February 1965

Opening Medley: **Glen Campbell** - Um, Um, Um, Um, Um, Um / **Donna Loren** - Blue Suede Shoes / **The Gauchos** - Down The Road Apiece / **Bobby Sherman** - Milk Cow Blues (End of Medley)
Glen Campbell and **Joey Cooper** - I've Got A Tiger By The Tail
Glen Campbell - It's Only Make Believe
The Gauchos - Out Of Sight
The Supremes - Eight Days A Week
Bobby Sherman - Don't Start Crying Now
The New Yorkers - Ain't That News
Freddie and The Dreamers - I'm Telling You Now
The Shindogs - I Don't Want To Spoil The Party
Donna Loren - With The Wind and The Rain In Your Hair
Jerry Naylor - I Found You
Stan Getz and **Ruth Price** - Telephone Song
The Supremes - Stop! In The Name Of Love
Jerry Naylor - I'll Take You Home
The Poets - Now We're Thru
Freddie and The Dreamers - Cut Across Shorty
Marianne Faithfull - Mary Ann *
The Barbarians - You've Got To Understand
The Supremes - You Can't Do That
Neil Sedaka - Happy Birthday Sweet Sixteen
Neil Sedaka - I Go Ape

JOEY COOPER: Pop singer and guitarist from Los Angeles, Calfornia. As well as a member of The Shindogs, he appeared 9 times on the show as a featured artist, this time performing a great version of Buck Owens' 'I've Got A Tiger By The Tail' alongside Glen Campbell.

THE NEW YORKERS: Jimmy Gresham, Douglas Brown and Roosevelt 'Rosey' Grier (b. 1932). Soul group from New York who recorded in Los Angeles. 'Ain't That News' was released as a single. Roosevelt 'Rosey' Grier was also a member of The Fearsome Foursome who appeared in Episode 20.

FREDDIE AND THE DREAMERS: A 1963 UK No. 2, 'I'm Telling You Now' topped the US charts when reissued in 1965. Eddie Cochran's 'Cut Across Shorty' is sung by burly bassist Pete Birrell.

JERRY NAYLOR: Jerry Naylor Jackson (b. 1939 - d. 2019). Rock 'n' Roll and Country singer from Chalk Mountain, Texas. 'I Found You' and The Drifters' 'I'll Take You Home' were both sides of his latest single. A former lead singer for The Crickets, this is the first of 4 'Shindig!' appearances.

STAN GETZ AND RUTH PRICE: Stanley Getz (b. 1927 - d. 1991 - saxophone) and Ruth Price (b. 1938 - vocals). Jazz duo. This is one of those occasional 'Shindig!' performances that leaves the audience totally nonplussed.

THE SUPREMES: 'Stop! In The Name Of Love' was a US No. 1 and UK No. 7.

THE POETS: George Gallacher (b. 1943 - d. 2012 - vocals), Hume Paton (Hume Michael Paton, b. 1945 - d. 2011 - guitar), Tony Myles (b. 1943 - guitar), John Dawson (b. 1944 - d. 2012 - bass) and Alan Weir (b. 1943 - d. 2010 - drums). Rhythm 'n' Blues and Pop group from Glasgow, Scotland, UK. 'Now We're Thru' was a No. 31 UK hit.

MARIANNE FAITHFULL: 'Mary Ann' is a track from the US 'Go Away From My World' and UK 'Come My Way' albums.

THE BARBARIANS: Victor 'Moulty' Moulton (drums and vocals), Ronnie Enos (guitar), Bruce Benson (guitar) and Jerry Causi (bass). Garage band from Cape Cod, Massachusetts. A group notable for drummer and singer Victor Moulton's missing left hand (he used a prosthetic hook), 'You've Got To Understand' was the B-side of their debut single.

NEIL SEDAKA: 1961's 'Happy Birthday Sweet Sixteen' was a US No. 6 and UK No. 3 hit, and 1958's 'I Go Ape' was a US No. 42 and UK No. 9. A fine performer, despite looking old enough to be the father of many performers on the show.

L R: The Supremes; Jerry Naylor; The Poets, Marianne Faithfull; The Barbarians; Nell Sedaka

Episode 26: 3rd March 1965

Opening Medley: **Bobby Sherman** - All Day and All Of The Night / **Suzie Kaye** - Really Saying Something / **Roy Clark** - Shake / **Jerry Cole** and **Russ Titleman** - Little Things / **Joe Tex** - Keep On Keeping On / **The Shindogs** and **The Gauchos** - Eight Days A Week

Suzie Kaye - Jerk and Twine

The Shindogs - Midnight Special

Little Eva - Let's Turkey Trot

Roy Clark - Lumberjack Man

Dave Berry - My Baby Left Me *

The Shindig Dancers - Busy Signal

Little Eva - I Want You To Be My Boy

Bobby Sherman - Goodnight

The Gauchos - Everyday

Joe Tex - Hold What You've Got

Jay and The Americans - Let's Lock The Door (and Throw Away The Key)

John Andrea - I'm Coming Home

The Rolling Stones - Heart Of Stone *

Roy Clark - The Wind Always Blows In Chicago

The Shindogs - A Big Hunk 'O Love

Johnny Tillotson - Angel

Jay and The Americans - Medley: At The Club / Come A Little Bit Closer

Little Eva - The Loco-motion

The Rolling Stones - Susie Q *

Bobby Sherman - Yeah, Yeah

The Chambers Brothers - People Get Ready

Joe Tex and **Darlene Love** - Yes Indeed

SUZIE KAYE: Susan Helene Klein (b. 1941 - d. 2008). Actress and singer from New York City.

THE SHINDOGS: The 'Shindig!' house band, the most common line-up was Delaney Bramlett (guitar and vocals), James Burton (guitar), Joey Cooper (bass), Glen D. Hardin (piano) and Chuck Blackwell (drums), though membership was flexible, with musicians coming and going. They appeared on the vast majority of 'Shindig!' Episodes.

LITTLE EVA: Eva Narcissus Boyd (b. 1943 - d. 2003). Rhythm 'n' Blues and Pop singer from Belhaven, North Carolina. 1963's 'Let's Turkey Trot' was a No. 20 US Pop hit, No. 16 R&B and No. 13 in the UK, and her debut 1962 single 'The Loco-Motion' got to No. 1 in both US Pop and R&B, as well as No. 2 in the UK.

DAVE BERRY: David Holgate Grundy (b. 1941). Rhythm 'n' Blues and Pop singer from Sheffield, Yorkshire, UK. 'My Baby Left Me' was a No. 37 UK hit. This is the first of 4 'Shindig!' appearances.

JOE TEX: Joseph Arrington Jr. (b. 1935 - d. 1982). Rhythm 'n' Blues and Soul singer from Rogers, Texas. 'Hold What You've Got' was a US Pop No. 5 and R&B No. 1. This is the first of 2 'Shindig!' appearances

JAY AND THE AMERICANS: 'Come A Little Closer' is another performance of their No. 3 hit, and 'Let's Lock The Door (and Throw Away The Key)' was a US No. 11.

THE ROLLING STONES: Again taped in London on 12th December 1964, The Rolling Stones' revival of Dale Hawkins' 'Susie Q' is a track from the US '12 x 5' and the UK 'The Rolling Stones No. 2' albums. 'Heart Of Stone' is a repeat of the performance in Episode 20.

L-R: Suzie Kaye; The Rolling Stones; Joe Tex; Jay and The Americans; Little Eva; Dave Berry

Episode 27: 10th March 1965

The Beau Brummels, **Donna Loren**, **Bobby Sherman**, **Mickey Rooney Jr.** and **Dobie Gray** - Rock and Roll Music
Donna Loren - I'm Ready
The Righteous Brothers - This Little Girl Of Mine
The Everly Brothers - Wake Up Little Susie
The Shindogs - I'm A Loser
Aretha Franklin - Can't You Just See Me?
Mickey Rooney Jr. - Forty Days
Donna Loren and **Bobby Sherman** - Just One Look
Dobie Gray - The 'In' Crowd
The Beau Brummels - Laugh, Laugh
Aretha Franklin and **Ray Johnson** - Mockingbird
The Shindogs - King Of The Road
Bill Medley - Old Man River
The Shindig Dancers (including **Maria Ghava**) - Give Him A Great Big Kiss
The Beau Brummels - Queen Of The Hop
John Andrea - Volare
The Drifters - At The Club
The Everly Brothers - That'll Be The Day
Bobby Sherman - Somebody To Love
The Everly Brothers - Bird Dog
Tony Bennett - Who Can I Turn To (When Nobody Needs Me) + I Guess I'll Have To Change My Plan
The Righteous Brothers - Ko Ko Mo

THE RIGHTEOUS BROTHERS: This was The Righteous Brothers' first 'Shindig!' appearance in two months as Bill Medley had been ill.

THE EVERLY BROTHERS: 1957's 'Wake Up Little Susie' got to No. 1 in US Pop, C&W and R&B and No. 6 in the UK, their latest single 'That'll Be The Day' stalled at No. 111 in the US and No. 30 in the UK, and 1958's 'Bird Dog' was a US Pop No. 2, C&W No. 1, R&B No. 2 and UK No. 2.

ARETHA FRANKLIN: Another performance of her No. 96 hit 'Can't You Just See Me'.

DOBIE GRAY: Lawrence Darrow Brown (b. 1940 - d. 2011). Soul and pop singer from Simonton, Texas. 'The 'In' Crowd' was a US Pop No. 13, R&B No. 11 and UK No. 25. This is the first of 2 'Shindig!' appearances.

THE BEAU BRUMMELS: Sal Valentino (Salvatore Spampinato, b. 1942 - vocals and tambourine), Ron Elliott (Ronald Charles Elliott, b. 1943 - guitar and vocals), Declan Mulligan (John Declan Mulligan, b. 1938 - guitar, harmonica and vocals), Ron Meagher (b. 1941 - bass and vocals) and John Petersen (John Louis Petersen, b. 1942 - d. 2007 - drums and vocals). Folk-Rock band from San Francisco, California. 'Laugh, Laugh' was a US No. 15. This is the first of 2 'Shindig!' appearances.

THE DRIFTERS: Johnny Moore (b. 1934 - d. 1998), Charlie Thomas (b. 1937), Gene Pearson and Johnny Terry. Rhythm 'n' Blues, Soul and Pop vocal group. A US Pop No. 43 and R&B No.10, 'At The Club' eventually got to No. 3 in the UK when reissued in 1972.

TONY BENNETT: Anthony Dominick Benedetto (b. 1926). Pop, Swing and Jazz singer from Queens, New York City. 'Who Can I Turn To (When Nobody Needs Me)' was a US Pop No. 33 and AC (Adult Contemporary) No. 3.

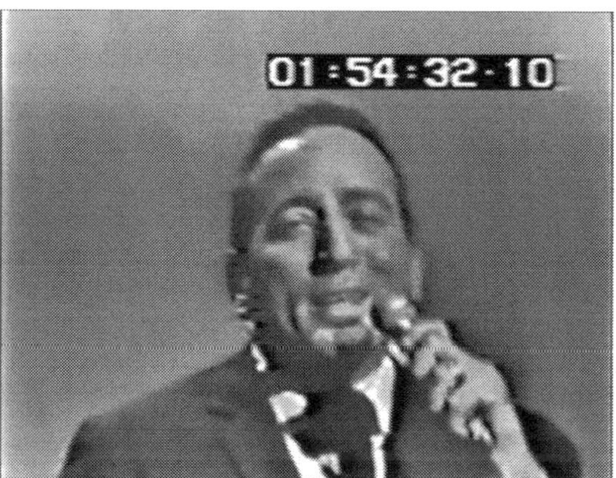

L-R: Aretha Franklin; Dobie Gray; The Beau Brummels; The Drifters; The Everly Brothers; Tony Bennett

Episode 28: 24th March 1965

Opening Medley: **Dick and Dee Dee** - Do You Wanna Dance? / **Shirley Ellis** - The Name Game / **Bobby Sherman** - King Creole (End of Medley)
The Shindogs and **The Ray Pohlman Band** - Shotgun
Medley: **Shirley Ellis** and **Jackie Wilson** - Gonna Mess Up A Good Thing / **Dick and Dee Dee** - Be My Baby
The Ray Polman Band and **The Wellingtons** - Rah, Rah, Shindig!
The Trade Winds - New York's A Lonely Town
The Blossoms - Peaches 'N' Cream
The Shindogs - Baby Please Don't Go
Donna Loren - Goldfinger
The Standells - Don't Let Me Be Misunderstood
The Shindig Dancers with **Ray Pohlman** - South Street
The Shindogs - I've Got A Tiger By The Tail
The Wellingtons - If I Fell
Jewel Akens - The Birds and The Bees
Dick and Dee Dee - How Do You Do It
Jackie Wilson - Danny Boy
Bobby Goldsboro - Little Things
Shirley Ellis - The Clapping Song
Bobby Sherman - Hello Mary Lou
The Standells - Come Home
Jackie Wilson - Sing (and Tell the Blues So Long)
Glen Campbell - Do The Clam

SHIRLEY ELLIS: Shirley Marie O'Garra (b. 1929 - d. 2005). Pop and Soul singer from The Bronx, New York. 'The Name Game' peaked at No. 3 in US Pop and No. 4 in R&B, and 'The Clapping Song' got to US Pop No. 8, R&B No. 16 and UK No. 6.

RAY POHLMAN: Merlyn Ray Pohlman (b. 1930 - d. 1990). Session bassist and guitarist, and Musical Director of 'The Shindogs'.

DICK AND DEE DEE: Not to be confused with The Ronettes' classic, 'Be My Baby' reached No. 87 in the US charts.

THE TRADE WINDS: Members include Peter Anders (Peter Andreoli, b. 1941 - d. 2016) and Vincent Poncia (b. 1942). Pop group from Providence, Rhode Island. 'New York's A Lonely Town' was a US No. 32 hit.

DONNA LOREN: Proving her versatility, 'Goldfinger' is almost as impressive as Shirley Bassey's hit version.

THE STANDELLS: Larry Tamblyn (guitar and keyboards), Tony Valentino (Emilio Tony Belilissimo - guitar), Gary Lane (Gary McMillan, b. 1938 - 2014 - bass) and Dick Dodd (drums and vocals). Pop and Garage group from Los Angeles, California.

THE SHINDIG DANCERS: 'South Street' was a 1963 hit for The Orlons.

JEWEL AKENS: Another performance of his US No. 3 hit.

JACKIE WILSON: His latest single, 'Danny Boy' was a US Pop No. 94 and R&B No. 25 hit, and 'Sing (and Tell the Blues So Long)' was a 1962 B-side.

BOBBY GOLDSBORO: Robert Charles Goldsboro (b. 1941). Pop and country singer from Marianna, Florida. 'Little Things' was a US No. 13. This is the first of 2 'Shindig!' appearances.

GLEN CAMPBELL: 'Do The Clam' was Elvis Presley's current hit, from his 17th movie 'Girl Happy'.

L-R: The Trade Winds; The Blossoms; The Standells; Jackie Wilson; Bobby Goldsboro; Shirley Ellis

Episode 29: 31st March 1965

Opening Medley: **The Wellingtons** - It's A Big Wonderful World / **Adam Faith** and **The Wellingtons** - Roll Over Beethoven / **The Blossoms** - Johnny B. Goode / **Bobby Sherman** - Sweet Little Sixteen / **Delaney Bramlett** - Memphis / **Joey Cooper** - Maybelline / **Sylvie Vartan** and **Chuck Berry** - Reelin' and Rockin' / **Chuck Berry** - Rock and Roll Music (End of Medley)
Adam Faith - Talk About Love
The Spats - Bony Maronie
Billy Fury - I'm Lost Without You *
Sylvie Vartan - Money (That's What I Want)
Chuck Berry - Back In The U.S.A.
Adam Faith - It's Alright
The Shindogs - The Race Is On
Jackie and Gayle - If I Loved You
Roosevelt 'Rosey' Grier - It's Not Unusual
Jerry Cole and **The Shindig Band** - Come Over To My Place
The Blossoms, **The Wellingtons**, **Ray Pohlman** and **The Shindig Band** - Woe Tom
John Andrea - Loddy Lo
Jerry Mason - Viva Las Vegas
The Shindogs - Shakin' All Over
Jackie and Gayle - I'll Save The Last Dance For You
The Spats - Gator Tails and Monkey Ribs
Sylvie Vartan - Twist and Shout
The Blossoms - Land Of A Thousand Dances
Adam Faith - Lucille
Chuck Berry - Dear Dad
Bobby Sherman - It Hurts Me + Roberta
Adam Faith, **Bobby Sherman** and **Jackie and Gayle** - It Sounds Good To Me

CHUCK BERRY: Charles Edward Anderson Berry (b. 1926 - d. 2017). Rock 'n' Roll and Rhythm 'n' Blues singer and guitarist from St. Louis, Missouri. 'Reelin' and Rockin'' was the 1958 B-side of 'Sweet Little Sixteen', 'Rock and Roll Music' a 1957 US No. 8 Pop hit and R&B No. 6, his excellent latest single 'Dear Dad' peaked at No. 95, and 1959's 'Back In The U.S.A.' was a US Pop No. 37 and R&B No. 16.

BILLY FURY: Ronald Wycherley (b. 1940 - d. 1983). Rock 'n' Roll and Pop singer from Liverpool, UK. Highly popular in his homeland where he had more than 25 hits during 1959-1966, his slightly re-titled cover of Teddy Randazzo's 'Lost Without You' was a UK No. 16 but failed completely in the USA, just like all his other records.

ADAM FAITH: This is his 3rd 'Shindig!' performance of 'It's Alright'.

JERRY COLE: Again proving to be a far better guitarist than singer, his version of The Drifters' 'Come On Over To My Place' was issued as a non-charting single.

SYLVIE VARTAN: Sylvie Georges Vartanian (b. 1944). Bulgarian-born Pop and Yé-Yé singer from Paris, France. 'Twist and Shout' is performed in French.

THE SHINDOGS: Long regarded as a rock 'n' roll classic in the UK thanks to Johnny Kidd and The Pirates original, few viewers in the USA would've known 'Shakin' All Over'.

JACKIE AND GAYLE: A 1960 single by Damita Jo, 'I'll Save The Last Dance For You' was an "answer" record to The Drifters' 'Save The Last Dance For Me'.

THE SPATS: Dick Johnson (vocals), Myron Carpino (guitar), Bud Johnson (guitar), Ron Johnson (bass) Mike Sulsona (drums), Chuck Showalter (piano) and Bob Dennis (saxophone). Rock and Pop band from California. 'Gator Tails and Monkey Ribs' was their current single.

L-R: Adam Faith; Billy Fury; Sylvie Vartan; Chuck Berry; Jackie and Gayle; Jerry Mason

Episode 30: 7th April 1965

Opening Medley: **Glen Campbell** - Hot Dog / **The Wellingtons**, **The Blossoms** and **John Andrea** Rock Island Line / **Tina Turner**, **Marvin Gaye**, and **The Righteous Brothers** - Willie and The Hand Jive (End of Medley)
Medley: **The Wellingtons** - The Game Of Love / **Tina Turner** - Money (That's What I Want) / **Marvin Gaye** - I'll Be Doggone / **Tina Turner** - That'll Be The Day / **Bobby Hatfield** and **Donna Loren** - I Must Be Seeing Things / **Lesley Gore** - Look Of Love / **Bill Medley** - You've Lost That Lovin' Feeling / **Lesley Gore** - Gee Baby I'm Sorry / **Bobby Hatfield** - Teasing You / **Bobby Hatfield** - Tell Her No / **Bill Medley** - Leave My Woman Alone / **Bobby Hatfield** - I'm A Lover Not A Fighter / **The Wellingtons** - The Game Of Love (End of Medley)
Donna Loren - Got To Get You Off My Mind
Jimmy Clanton - Tired Of Waiting For You
The Blossoms - The Barracuda
The Shindogs - Shotgun
Medley: **Marvin Gaye** - Stubborn Kind Of Fellow / **Tina Turner** - Tell Her I'm Not Home / **Marvin Gaye** - Memphis / **Marvin Gaye** - Don't Let Me Be Misunderstood / **Tina Turner** - Tell The Truth / **The Wellingtons** - She Loves You (End of Medley)
Willy Nelson - I'm In Love With The Dancing Girl Working At the Metropole
John Andrea and **The Shindogs** - Sweet Little Sixteen
Delaney Bramlett - Jack O' Diamonds
Glen Campbell - Tomorrow Never Comes
Larry Hovis - Cherry Pie
Martha and The Vandellas - Nowhere To Run
Lesley Gore - All Of My Life
The Righteous Brothers - I Need Your Loving
Marvin Gaye - Can I Get A Witness

MARVIN GAYE: His latest single, 'I'll Be Doggone' got to No. 8 in US Pop and No. 1 in R&B, 1962's 'Stubborn Kind Of Fellow' was a US Pop No. 46 and R&B No. 8, and 1963's 'Can I Get A Witness' peaked at US Pop No. 22 and R&B No. 3. 'I'll Be Doggone' and 'Stubborn Kind Of Fellow' are performed here as parts of lengthy medleys.

TINA TURNER: Ike and Tina Turner's latest single, 'Tell Her I'm Not Home' was a US Pop No. 108 and R&B No. 33.

JIMMY CLANTON: (b. 1938). Pop singer from Raceland, Louisiana. The first of 2 'Shindig!' appearances, 'Tired Of Waiting For You' is a version of The Kinks' classic.

THE BLOSSOMS: The Blossoms do not feature Darlene Love in this episode, where she is replaced by an unknown temporary member.

WILLY NELSON: 'I'm In Love With The Dancing Girl Working At the Metropole' is another performance of his non-charting single.

GLEN CAMPBELL: 'Tomorrow Never Comes' is a 2nd performance of his minor US hit.

LARRY HOVIS: (b. 1936 - d. 2003). Actor and occasional singer, best remembered for appearing in 'Hogan's Heroes'.

MARTHA AND THE VANDELLAS: Martha Reeves (Martha Rose Reeves, b. 1941), Rosalind Ashford (Rosalind Ashford-Holmes, b. 1943) and Betty Kelly (Betty Kelley, b. 1944). Rhythm 'n' Blues and Soul vocal group from Detroit, Michigan. 'Nowhere To Run' was a US Pop No. 8, R&B No. 5 and UK No. 26.

LESLEY GORE: Lesley Sue Goldstein (b. 1946 - d. 2015). Pop singer from Brooklyn, New York. 'Look Of Love' was a US No. 27 hit, and 'All Of My Life' got to No. 71. This is the first of 2 'Shindig!' appearances.

L-R: Marvin Gaye and Tina Turner; Lesley Gore and Bill Medley; Donna Loren; Jimmy Clanton; Larry Hovis; Martha and The Vandellas

Episode 31: 14th April 1965

Opening Medley: **The Shindogs** - Shakin' All Over / **Donna Loren** and **The Wellingtons** - Talk About Love / **The Blossoms** - Peaches 'N' Cream / **Millie Small** - Be My Baby / **Jerry Lee Lewis** - Whole Lotta Shakin' Going On / **The Righteous Brothers** - Ko Ko Joe (End of Medley)

Bobby Hatfield - Come See

The Shindogs - Find My Way Back Home

Sounds Incorporated - Time For You

Neil Sedaka - Let The People Talk

Millie Small - I'm Blue

The Wellingtons - Bumble Bee

Glen Campbell - Wabash Cannonball

Anita Sheer - Cecilia

Jerry Lee Lewis - I Believe In You

Nino Tempo and April Stevens - Swing Me

The Blossoms - I Like It Like That

Donna Loren - Finger Poppin'

Anita Sheer - I'll Never Find Another You

Sounds Incorporated - Hall Of The Mountain King

Jerry Mason - For Mama

Neil Sedaka - Breaking Up Is Hard To Do

Millie Small - My Boy Lollipop

James Burton - Love Lost

The Righteous Brothers - Try To Find Another Man

Jerry Lee Lewis and **Neil Sedaka** - Take Me Out To The Ball Game

JERRY LEE LEWIS: 'Whole Lotta Shakin' Going On' is another performance of his giant hit, 'I Believe In You' was the B-side of his current single 'Baby, Hold Me Close', and 'Take Me Out To The Ball Game' is a song neither he or Neil Sedaka released on record. The fantastic piano solo in 'I Believe In You' has to be seen to be believed.

THE SHINDOGS: 'Find My Way Back Home' is a superb version of The Nashville Teens' UK hit at the time.

SOUNDS INCORPORATED: 'Time For You' b/w 'Hall Of The Mountain King' was the group's current single.

NEIL SEDAKA: 'Let The People Talk' stalled at No. 107 in the US charts, and 1962's 'Breaking Up Is Hard To Do' was a US No. 1 and UK No. 7.

MILLIE SMALL: Millicent Dolly May Small (b. 1947 - d. 2020). Ska and Blue Beat singer from Clarendon, Jamaica. 'My Boy Lollipop' got to No. 2 in both the US and UK. This is the first of 2 'Shindig!' appearances. 'Be My Baby' is the Dick and Dee Dee song, the studio version of her rather shrill cover of The Ikettes' 'I'm Blue' featured backing by The Spencer Davis Group, and 'My Boy Lollipop' features a saxophone solo here rather than the usual harmonica.

ANITA SHEER: (d. 1996). Folk and Flamenco artist from New York City. 'Cecilia' was the A-side of her 1st single, and 'I'll Never Find Another You' is a nice cover of The Seekers' big hit.

NINO TEMPO AND APRIL STEVENS: Antonino Lo Tempio (b. 1935) and Carol Lo Tempio (b. 1929). Pop duo from Niagara Falls, New York. 'Swing Me' was a very minor hit at No. 127 in the US charts.

THE BLOSSOMS: Originally by Chris Kenner, 'I Like It Like That' was a Top 10 US hit for The Dave Clark Five.

JAMES BURTON: Rock and Roll, Rockabilly and Country guitarist from Dubberly, Louisiana. Best remembered for his early work with Rick Nelson and later touring with Elvis Presley, he was a regular part of 'Shindig!' as an anonymous backing musician, also appearing 3 times as a featured artist. 'Love Lost' was his debut solo single.

L-R: Sounds Incorporated; Anita Sheer; Jerry Lee Lewis; Nino Tempo and April Stevens; Millie Small; Jerry Lee Lewis and Neil Sedaka

Episode 32: 21st April 1965

The Beach Boys - Do You Wanna Dance
Rita Pavone - Just Once More
Dick and Dee Dee - Freight Train + Be My Baby
Joe and Eddie - Swing Down Sweet Chariot
The Shangri-Las - Shout
Joey Cooper - Do The Clam + Love (Is You)
The Ikettes - Peaches 'N' Cream
The Shindogs - She's About A Mover
The Shangri-Las - Give Him A Great Big Kiss
Ian Whitcomb with **The Shangri-Las** - I'm A Loser
Ian Whitcomb - This Sporting Life
Carole Shelyne - The Girl With The Horned Rimmed Glasses
Cilla Black - I've Been Wrong Before
Rita Pavone - Your Baby's Gone Surfing
Joe and Eddie - All Night Long
The Shangri-Las - Out In The Streets
Wayne Fontana and The Mindbenders - Stop, Look and Listen *
The Ikettes - Camel Walk
The Beach Boys - Fun, Fun, Fun + Long Tall Texan + Please Let Me Wonder + Help Me, Rhonda
Rita Pavone - Eyes Of Mine
The Beach Boys - Their Hearts Were Full Of Spring
Joe and Eddie - There's A Meeting Here Tonite

THE BEACH BOYS: 'Do You Wanna Dance?' was a US No. 12 hit, 'Fun, Fun, Fun' No. 9, 'Please Let Me Wonder' (the flipside of 'Do You Wanna Dance?') No. 52, and 'Help Me, Rhonda' a US chart-topper and a UK No. 27.

RITA PAVONE: (b. 1945). Pop singer from Milan, Italy. 'Just Once More' was a US single release. This is the first of 2 'Shindig!' appearances. 'Your Baby's Gone Surfing' is performed in Italian.

JOE AND EDDIE: Joe Gilbert (b. 1941 - d. 1966) and Eddie Brown (Edward Roger Brown, b. 1941). Folk and Gospel duo from Berkeley, California. 'There's A Meeting Here Tonite' was the title track of their album of the same name.

THE SHANGRI-LAS: Mary Weiss (b. 1948), Marge Ganser (Marguerite Ganser, b. 1948 - d. 1996) and Mary Ann Ganser (b. 1948 - d. 1970). Girl group from Queens, New York City. 'Give Us A Great Big Kiss' got to No. 18 in the US charts, while the great 'Out In The Streets' peaked at No. 53. The Shangri-Las would make 1 further appearance on the show.

JOEY COOPER: 'Love (Is You)' was his latest single.

THE IKETTES: Robbie Montgomery (Robbie Marie Montgomery, b. 1940), Venetta Fields (Venetta Lee Fields (b. 1941) and Jessie Smith (b. 1941 - d. 2021). US Rhythm 'n' Blues and Soul vocal group who were also singers and dancers for Ike and Tina Turner. 'Peaches 'N' Cream' was a US Pop No. 36 and R&B No. 28, and 'Camel Walk' was a US Pop 107.

IAN WHITCOMB: Ian Timothy Whitcomb (b. 1941 - d. 2020). Rhythm 'n' Blues and Pop singer and pianist from Woking, Surrey, UK. 'This Sporting Life' was a US No. 100 hit. This is the first of 6 'Shindig!' performances.

CAROLE SHELYNE: Carole Stuppler (b. 1943 - d. 2015). Dancer, actress and singer from Brooklyn, New York, also known as Carolyne Barry. A 'Shindig!' dancing regular, this was her only appearance as a vocalist.

CILLA BLACK: Priscilla Maria Veronica White (b. 1943 - d. 2015). Pop singer from Liverpool, UK. Randy Newman's 'I've Been Wrong Before' was a No. 17 UK hit for her, but failed to chart in the US. This live version shows off her incredible vocal range.

WAYNE FONTANA AND THE MINDBENDERS: Wayne Fontana (Glyn Geoffrey Ellis, b. 1945 - d. 2020 - vocals), Eric Stewart (Eric Michael Stewart, b. 1945 - guitar and vocals), Bob Lang (Robert Francis Lang, b. 1946 - bass) and Ric Rothwell (Eric Rothwell, b. 1944 - drums). Beat Group from Manchester. 'Stop, Look and Listen' was a UK No. 37 hit.

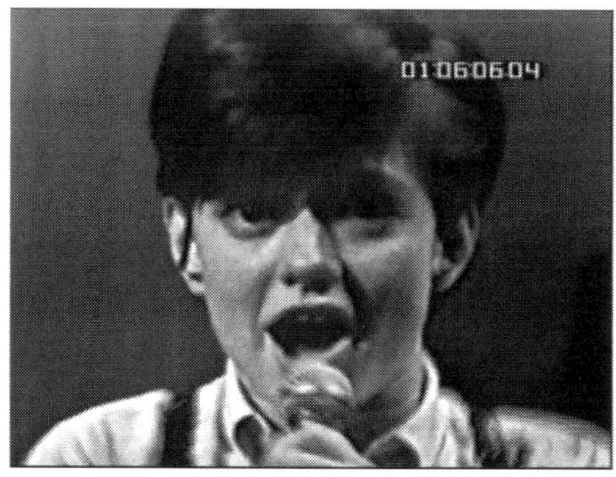

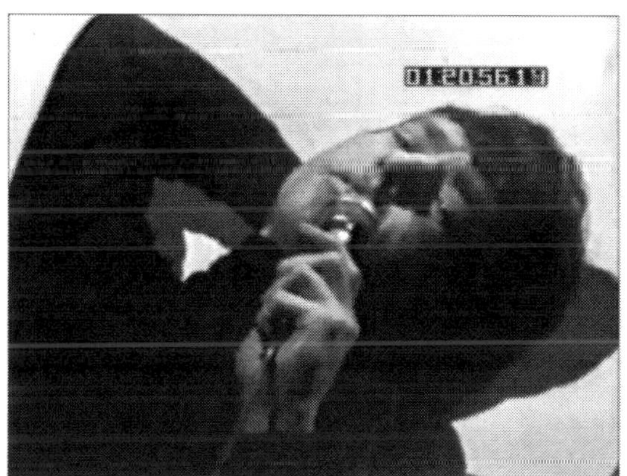

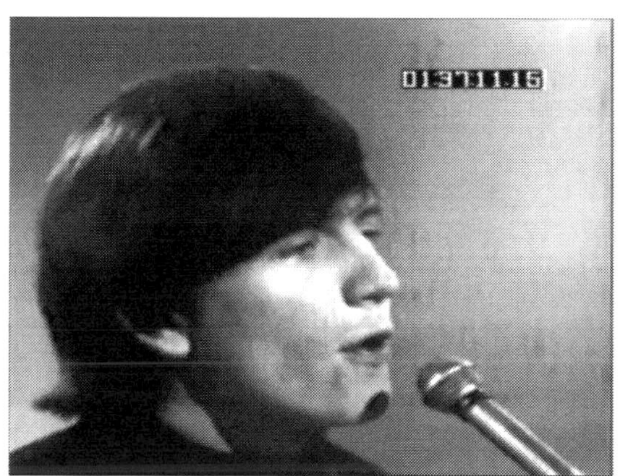

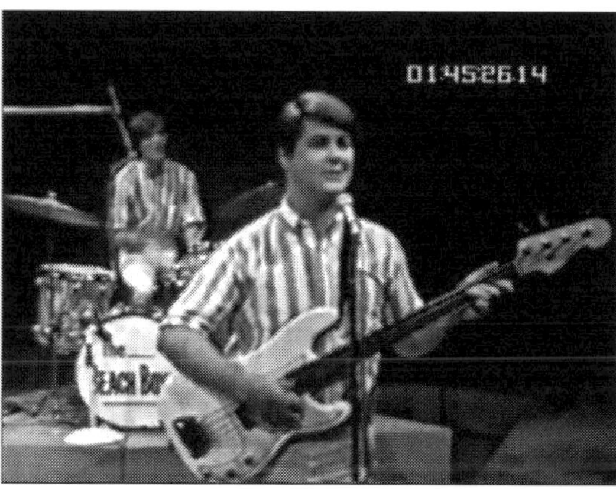

L-R: Rita Pavone; The Shangri-Las; Ian Whitcomb; Cilla Black; Wayne Fontana and The Mindbenders; The Beach Boys

Episode 33: 28th April 1965

Opening Medley: **Donna Loren**, **The Wellingtons**, and **The Blossoms** - Tutti Frutti / **Dick and Dee Dee** - The Birds Are For The Bees / **The Shindogs** - Dear Dad (End of Medley)
Bobby Sherman - School Day (Ring! Ring! Goes The Bell)
The Blossoms - All Around The World
Freddie and The Dreamers - If You Gotta Make A Fool Of Somebody *
Donna Loren - I Know A Place
Freddie and The Dreamers - I Understand (Just How You Feel) *
Sandie Shaw - Girl Don't Come *
Leroy Van Dyke - The Auctioneer
Manfred Mann - I Got My Mojo Working *
Dick and Dee Dee - Rockin' Pneumonia and The Boogie Woogie Flu
The Shindogs - My Baby Left Me
The Four Tops - Baby I Need Your Loving
Bobby Sherman and **Donna Loren** - Heebie Jeebies
Leroy Van Dyke - My Heart Keeps Hangin' On
Bettye Swann - The Man Who Said No
Manfred Mann - Come Tomorrow *
Sandie Shaw - I'd Be Far Better Off Without You *
The Four Tops - Ask The Lonely
The Shindogs - She's About A Mover
The Wellingtons - You Can't Sit Down

THE BLOSSOMS: Their performance of Little Richard's 'All Around The World' features Billy Preston's prominent organ.

FREDDIE AND THE DREAMERS: The group's light-hearted cover of James Ray's 'If You Gotta Make A Fool Of Somebody' was a No. 3 UK hit in 1963 but flopped in the US, and 'I Understand (Just How You Feel)' got to No. 5 in the UK and No. 36 in the US.

SANDIE SHAW: 'Girl Don't Come' is a repeat of the performance in Episode 18, while 'I'd Be Far Better Off Without You' is that single's B-side.

LEROY VAN DYKE: Leroy Frank Van Dyke (b. 1929). Country singer and guitarist from Mora, Missouri. 'The Auctioneer' was a US Pop No. 19 and C&W No. 9. This was the first of 2 'Shindig!' appearances.

MANFRED MANN: 'Come Tomorrow' stalled at No. 50 in the US but got to No. 4 in the UK.

DICK AND DEE DEE: 'Rockin' Pneumonia and The Boogie Woogie Flu' again features lots of Billy Preston's impressive organ.

THE SHINDOGS: 'My Baby Left Me' includes some impressive guitar work by James Burton, something he'd later do behind Elvis Presley, the person who made the song famous.

THE FOUR TOPS: Levi Stubbs (Levi Stubbles, b. 1936 - d. 2008), Abdul 'Duke' Fakir (b. 1935), Renaldo 'Obie' Benson (b. 1936 - d. 2005) and Lawrence Payton (Lawrence Albert Payton, b. 1938 - d. 1997). Soul and pop vocal group from Detroit, Michigan. 'Baby I Need Your Loving' was a US No. 11 hit, and 'Ask The Lonely' got to No. 24 in US Pop and No. 9 in R&B. This is the first of 2 'Shindig!' appearances.

BETTYE SWAN: Betty Jean Champion (b. 1944). Soul singer from Shreveport, Louisiana. 'The Man Who Said No' was her 2nd single.

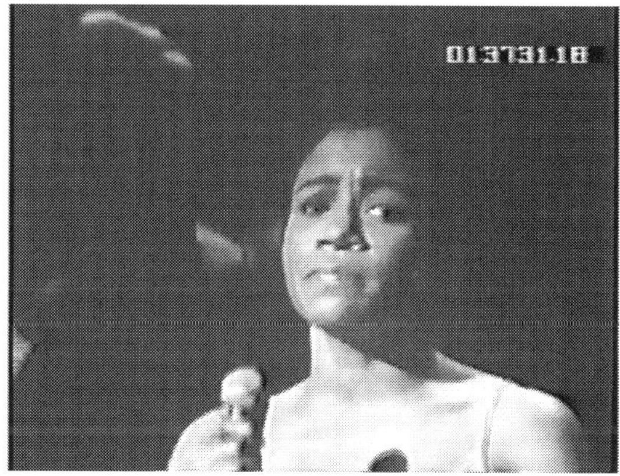

L-R: Freddie and The Dreamers; Sandie Shaw; Leroy Van Dyke; Manfred Mann; The Four Tops; Bettye Swann

Episode 34: 5th May 1965

Opening Medley: **Joey Cooper** - Blue Suede Shoes / **The Blossoms** Got A Lot O' Livin' To Do / **Glen Campbell** - Big Hunk O' Love / **The Wellingtons** - I Need Your Love Tonight / **Sonny and Cher** - I Got Stung / **The Chambers Brothers** - Hard Headed Woman (End of Medley)
Delaney Bramlett - That's Alright Mama
The Wellingtons, **The Blossoms** and **The Chambers Brothers** - Wear My Ring Around Your Neck
Ray Peterson - Can't Help Falling In Love
Linda Gail Lewis - Don't Be Cruel
Willy Nelson - Hound Dog
Maria Ghava - Hey, Memphis
Joey Cooper - Mean Woman Blues
Sonny and Cher - Let Me Be Your Teddy Bear
Jimmy Boyd - Hot Dog
Ray Peterson - It's Now Or Never
The Chambers Brothers - Jailhouse Rock
The Shindig Dancers - Party
Joey Cooper - Crawfish
Sonny and Cher - All Shook Up
Glen Campbell - Trouble
Ray Peterson - Heartbreak Hotel
Cher - Wooden Heart
The Blossoms - Shake Rattle And Roll
Jimmy Boyd - Poor Boy
Sonny and Cher - Treat Me Nice
Glen Campbell - Surrender
Linda Gail Lewis - Crying In The Chapel
The Shindogs - King Creole
Joey Cooper - Blue Suede Shoes (reprise)

SONNY AND CHER: Sonny and Cher made some wonderful records, but it is disappointing they are the biggest act 'Shindig!' could come up with for their Elvis Presley Special, particularly when his songs are so ill-suited to their Folk-Pop style.

DELANEY BRAMLETT: The best thing about 'That's Alright Mama', and indeed the whole programme, is James Burton's great pickin'.

MARIA GHAVA: Dancer (and not much of a singer) from Los Angeles who regularly appeared on 'Shindig!'. Originally recorded by LaVern Baker in 1961, 'Hey, Memphis' was an "answer" record to Elvis Presley's 'Little Sister'.

JIMMY BOYD: Jimmy Devon Boyd (b. 1939 - d. 2009). Pop and Country singer and actor from Colton, California.

LINDA GAIL LEWIS: Jerry Lee's little sister is as good as anyone else on this admittedly mediocre Episode, particularly on 'Crying In The Chapel'.

L-R: The Chambers Brothers; Ray Peterson; Linda Gail Lewis; Maria Ghava; Sonny and Cher; Glen Campbell

Episode 35: 12th May 1965

Opening Medley: **Russ Titleman** and **The Righteous Brothers** - Don't Bring Me Down / Two Drummers (**Charles Blackwell** of **The Shindogs** and the drummer from **The Ray Pohlman Band**) - Drum Solo / **Dick and Dee Dee** - Baby, Please Don't Go / **The Shindogs** and **The Olympics** - Jenny, Jenny (End of Medley)
Medley: **The Olympics** - (Baby) Hully Gully / **The Righteous Brothers** - Walking The Dog / **The Blossoms** - (Baby) Hully Gully / **The Shindogs** - Walking The Dog + The Last Time / **The Olympics** - (Baby) Hully Gully (reprise, End of Medley)
Bobby Sherman - Silhouettes
Dick and Dee Dee - It's Gonna Be Alright
The Moody Blues - I'll Go Crazy *
Brenda Holloway - When I'm Gone
The Righteous Brothers - Just Once In My Life
The Blossoms - Goodbye, So Long
Bach Yen - Pas Touch
Brenda Holloway - He's Coming Home
Delaney Bramlett and **The Shindogs** - High Blood Pressure
Dino, Desi and Billy - I'm A Fool
Jerry Mason - My Babe
Dick and Dee Dee - Hello Josephine
Russ Titleman - Bright Lights, Big City
The Shindogs - Gloria
The Moody Blues - Go Now *
The Righteous Brothers - I'm A Hog For You Baby
The Olympics - Good Lovin'

THE OLYMPICS: Walter Ward, Eddie Lewis, Charles Fizer, Walter Hammond and Melvin King. Rhythm 'n' Blues and Soul group from Los Angeles, California. 1960's '(Baby) Hully Gully' was a US No. 72, and their latest record 'Good Lovin'' a US No. 81.

THE MOODY BLUES: 'Go Now' is a repeat of the performance in Episode 24, and James Brown's 'I'll Go Crazy' is a song from their debut album.

BRENDA HOLLOWAY: (b. 1946). Soul singer from Los Angeles, California. 'When I'm Gone' was a US Pop No. 25 and R&B No. 12, while 'He's Coming Home' is a gender-reversed version of The Zombies' 'She's Coming Home'. This is the first of 2 'Shindig!' performances.

THE RIGHTEOUS BROTHERS: Their current single, 'Just Once In My Life' peaked at No. 9 in the US charts.

BACH YEN: Quách Thị Bạch Yến (b. 1942). Singer from Vietnam. 'Pas Touch' was released as a single.

DINO, DESI AND BILLY: Members were Dean Paul Martin Jr. (b. 1951 - d. 1987 - vocals and bass), Desiderio Alberto Arnaz IV (b. 1953 - vocals and drums) and William Ernest Hinsche (b. 1951 - vocals and guitar). Pop group from California. 'I'm A Fool' got to No. 17 in the US charts.

L-R: Dick and Dee Dee; The Moody Blues; Brenda Holloway; The Blossoms; Dino, Desi and Billy; The Olympics

Episode 36: 19th May 1965

Opening Medley: **The Righteous Brothers** - This Little Girl Of Mine / **Donna Loren** and **Bobby Sherman** - Sticks and Stones / **The Blossoms** - Guess Who / **The Wellingtons** - Hit The Road, Jack / **Ray Charles** - I Can't Stop Loving You (End of Medley)
Billy Preston - Instrumental
Donna Loren - Cycle Set
Bobby Sherman - Hey Little Girl
The Wellingtons - Little Old Lady From Pasadena
Dinah Lee - You Don't Talk About Love
Ray Peterson - House Without Windows
Joe Williams - I'm Sticking With You Baby
The Zombies - It's Alright With Me *
Glen Campbell - Guess I'm Dumb
The Shindogs - Hippy Hippy Shake
Donna Loren - Into My Heart
Ray Charles - I've Got A Woman
The Righteous Brothers - Bring It On Home To Me
Dinah Lee - Oh, Boy!
The Zombies - Summertime *
George Soulé - I Love The Way You Love
The Righteous Brothers - Sticks And Stones
Bobby Sherman - Well.... Alright
Ray Charles - Georgia On My Mind
Ray Charles with **The Righteous Brothers** and **The Blossoms** - What'd I Say

RAY CHARLES: Ray Charles Robinson (b. 1930 - d. 2004). Rhythm 'n' Blues, Soul and Jazz singer and pianist from Albany, Georgia. 'I Can't Stop Loving You' was a 1962 US Pop, US R&B and UK No. 1, 1954's 'I've Got A Woman' topped the US R&B charts, 'Georgia On My Mind' got to No. 1 in US Pop, No. 3 in R&B and No. 24 in the UK in 1960, and 'What'd I Say' was No. 6 US Pop and No. 1 R&B in 1959.

BILLY PRESTON: William Everett Preston (b. 1946 - d. 2006). Rhythm 'n' Blues, Soul and Gospel singer and keyboardist from Houston, Texas. A 'Shindig!' regular, he appeared on the show 24 times.

DINAH LEE: Diane Marie Jacobs (b. 1943). Pop singer from Christchurch, New Zealand. The first of 2 'Shindig!' appearances, for this one she arrives on the back of a moped with Jack Good.

JOE WILLIAMS: Joseph Goreed (b. 1918 - d. 1999). Jazz and Blues singer from Cordele, Georgia. Not to be confused with singer and guitarist Big Joe Williams, 'I'm Sticking With You, Baby' is a track from his 1964 album 'Me and The Blues'.

THE ZOMBIES: Both songs are from their US debut 'The Zombies'.

GLEN CAMPBELL: 'Guess I'm Dumb' was his latest, non-charting, single.

GEORGE SOULÉ: George Halbert Soulé Jr. (b. 1945). Soul singer and songwriter from Meridian, Mississippi.

BOBBY SHERMAN: 'Well.... Alright' is a great stomping update of a Buddy Holly song.

L-R: Donna Loren; Dinah Lee; Joe Williams; The Zombies; Ray Charles, George Soulé

Episode 37: 26th May 1965

Opening Medley: **Bobby Sherman** with **Len and Glenn, Brady and Grady** - Reelin' and Rockin' / **Sonny and Cher** - Whole Lotta Shakin' Going On / **The Blossoms** and **The Wellingtons** - Johnny B. Goode / **Joey Cooper** and **Delaney Bramlett** - The Peppermint Twist / **The Rolling Stones** - Down The Road Apiece (End of Medley)
Jimmie Rodgers - Honeycomb
Jackie DeShannon - Something's Got A Hold Of Me
Len and Glenn, Brady and Grady - I Think I'm Getting Wiser Everyday
Adam Wade - Garden In The Rain
The Rolling Stones - Little Red Rooster
The Wellingtons - Short, Shorts
The Shindogs - Ticket To Ride
Howlin' Wolf - How Many More Years
The Explosions - Work With Me, Annie
The Rolling Stones - The Last Time
Sonny and Cher - We're Gonna Make It
Bobby Sherman - Ready Teddy
Jackie DeShannon - What The World Needs Now Is Love
Rick Lancelot - Doctor Feelgood
The Rolling Stones - Play With Fire
Jimmie Rodgers - Woman From Liberia
Len and Glenn, Brady and Grady - Love Me
The Rolling Stones - (I Can't Get No) Satisfaction

THE ROLLING STONES: In live vocal performances taped 6 days earlier, 'Down The Road Apiece' is a track from the US 'The Rolling Stones, Now!' and the UK 'The Rolling Stones No. 2', Howlin' Wolf's 'Little Red Rooster' was a UK chart-topping single and a track from the US 'The Rolling Stones, Now!' album, 'The Last Time' was a single that got to No. 9 in the US and No. 1 in the UK as well as appearing on the US 'Out Of Our Heads' album, 'Play With Fire' was the UK and US B-side of 'The Last Time', and, here in a radically different early arrangement with harmonica, '(I Can't Get No) Satisfaction' topped both the US and UK singles charts and appeared on the US 'Out Of Our Heads' album. 'Little Red Rooster' features Mick on what looks like the set for a horror movie, while 'Play With Fire' has the entire band (minus instruments) on a vintage car.

JIMMIE RODGERS: James Frederick Rodgers (b. 1933 - d. 2021). Country and Pop singer from Camas, Washington. 1957's 'Honeycomb' was a US Pop No. 1, C&W No. 7 and R&B No. 1, while 'Woman From Liberia' was a 1960 flop. This is the first of 2 'Shindig!' performances.

JACKIE DESHANNON: Her current single, 'What The World Needs Now Is Love' peaked at US No. 7, while a cover of Etta James' 'Something's Got A Hold On Me' demonstrates this artist's great versatility.

LEN AND GLENN, BRADY AND GRADY: Brady and Grady are probably Brady and Grady Sneed, a Soul duo who released several obscure singles.

ADAM WADE: Patrick Henry Wade (b. 1935). Pop and Easy Listening singer from Pittsburgh, Pennsylvania. 'Garden In The Rain' was his latest single.

HOWLIN' WOLF: Chester Arthur Burnett (b. 1910 - d. 1976). Blues and Rhythm 'n' Blues singer, guitarist and harmonica player from White Station, Mississippi. 1951's 'How Many More Years' got to No. 4 in the US R&B charts.

THE EXPLOSIONS: Soul group from New Orleans. Their fine revival of Hank Ballard and The Midniters 'Work With Me, Annie' was their debut single.

RICK LANCELOT: Ricky Lancelotti (b. 1944 - d. 1980). Rhythm 'n' Blues singer from New Jersey. This is the first of 2 'Shindig!' appearances.

L-R: Sonny and Cher; Jimmie Rodgers; Jackie DeShannon; Adam Wade; Howlin' Wolf; The Rolling Stones

Episode 38: 2nd June 1965

Opening Medley: **Bobby Sherman** and **Diane Renay** - Peggy Sue / **The Blossoms** and **Wellingtons** - Keep A Knockin' / **The Righteous Brothers** - Be-Bop-A-Lula
Major Lance - Ain't That A Shame
Bobby Sherman with **Delaney Bramlett** and **Joey Cooper** - Wooly Bully
Linda Carr - Da Doo Run Run
The Shindogs - It's Gonna Be Alright
The Righteous Brothers - Ko Ko Joe
Diane Renay - Dum Dum
Bobby Sherman - Yeh Yeh
The Blossoms - Down By The Riverside
Delaney Bramlett - Gambling Man
The Wellingtons - Three Cool Cats
Bobby Sherman, **The Blossoms** and **The Wellingtons** - Peppermint Twist
Linda Carr - What'd I Say
Marianne Faithfull - Once I Had A Sweetheart *
Patty Duke - Don't Just Stand There
Major Lance - The Monkey Time
The Shindogs - Country Music Is Here To Stay
The Righteous Brothers - You'll Never Walk Alone + Big Boy Pete
Patty Duke - Everything But Love
Billy Preston - Lucille
The Righteous Brothers - Big Boy Pete
Linda Carr - See See Rider

LINDA CARR: (b. 1944). Soul singer from Los Angeles, California. This is the first of 2 appearances on the show.

DIANE RENAY: Renee Diane Kushner (b. 1945). Pop singer from Philadelphia, Pennsylvania. 'Dum Dum' was a 1962 hit for Brenda Lee.

MARIANNE FAITHFULL: 'Mary Ann' is a track from her UK 'Come My Way' album.

PATTY DUKE: Anna Marie Duke (b. 1946 - d. 2016). Singer and actress from New York City. 'Don't Just Stand There' was a No. 8 US hit. This is the first of 2 'Shindig!' appearances.

MAJOR LANCE: (b. 1939 - d. 1994). Rhythm 'n' Blues and Soul singer from Winterville, Mississippi. 'The Monkey Time' was a US Pop No. 8 and R&B No. 2. This is the first of 2 'Shindig!' appearances.

L-R: Major Lance; Linda Carr; Diane Renay; Marianne Faithfull; Patty Duke; Billy Preston

Episode 39: 9th June 1965

Opening Medley: **Jackie and Gayle** - Iko Iko / **The Blossoms** - Don't Hang Up / **The Wellingtons** and **Bobby Sherman** - The Bristol Stomp / **Billy Preston** - Baby Face / **The Everly Brothers** - Gone, Gone, Gone (End of Medley)
Billy Preston - Log Cabin
Piccola Pupa - Breakaway
Glen Campbell - Tom Dooley
Clydie King - The Thrill Is Gone
Sandie Shaw - (There's) Always Something There To Remind Me *
Jackie and Gayle - That's How It Goes
Bobby Sherman - Country Boy
Darlene Love - Didn't It Rain?
Jimmy Clanton - Hurting Each Other
The Wellingtons (with **The Shindig Dancers**) - Sunglasses
Bettye LaVette - Let Me Down Easy
The Everly Brothers - Great Balls Of Fire
Bobby Hatfield - Out Of Sight
Piccola Pupa - Skateboard
The Vocals - Lonesome Mood
Bobby Sherman and **The Wellingtons** - Good Golly Miss Molly
The Everly Brothers and **The Righteous Brothers** - Slippin' and Slidin'
Billy Preston - Breathless
The Wellingtons, **The Blossoms**, **Jackie and Gayle**, **The Righteous Brothers** and **Bobby Sherman** - Camel Walk
Glen Campbell - Fort Worth Jail
The Righteous Brothers - I've Been Working On The Railroad
The Everly Brothers - The Price Of Love

THE EVERLY BROTHERS: 'Gone, Gone, Gone' was a US No. 31 and UK No. 36, Jerry Lee Lewis' 'Great Balls Of Fire' is a song they never recorded, 'Slippin' and Slidin'' is from their album 'Rock'n Soul', and their current single 'The Price Of Love' got to No. 104 in the US and all the way to No. 2 in the UK.

BILLY PRESTON: 'Log Cabin' was Billy's latest single.

PICCOLA PUPA: Giuliana Crimilde Coverlizza (b. 1951). Singer and actress from Genoa, Italy. A song written by 'Shindig!' regular Jackie DeShannon and Jimmy O'Neill's wife Sharon Sheeley, 'Breakaway' was first released by Irma Thomas.

CLYDIE KING: 'The Thrill Is Gone' was a 1965 single.

SANDIE SHAW: This is a repeat from Episode 18.

JACKIE AND GAYLE: 'That's How It Goes' was their latest single.

BOBBY SHERMAN: 'Country Boy' was a 1960 hit for Fats Domino.

JIMMY CLANTON: 'Hurting Each Other' was his current single.

BETTYE LAVETTE: Betty Jo Haskins (b. 1946). Soul singer from Muskegon, Michigan. 'Let Me Down Easy' got to No. 103 in the US Pop charts and No. 20 in R&B.

THE VOCALS: Lamont McLemore, Marilyn McCoo (b. 1943), Harry Elston, Fritz Baskett and Lawrence Summers. Pop and Soul vocal group from Los Angeles, California. The single 'Lonesome Mood' featured Ray Charles on piano.

L-R: Piccola Pupa; Clydie King; Jimmy Clanton; Bettye LaVette; The Everly Brothers, The Vocals

Episode 40: 16th June 1965

Opening Medley: **The Everly Brothers** - Wake Up Little Susie / **Dick and Dee Dee** - Should We Tell Him / **Gary Brento Weis** - What'd I Say / **Gerry and The Pacemakers** - Slow Down (End of Medley)
Petula Clark - In Love
Gary Lewis and The Playboys - Count Me In
The Wellingtons - Wonderful World
Dick and Dee Dee with **Gerry Marsden** - A Shot Of Rhythm and Blues
Billy Preston - Little Sally Walker
P.J. Proby - Hold Me
Gary Brento Weis - Lover Man
Cliff Bennett and The Rebel Rousers - I Can't Stand It *
Dick St. John Gosting with **Gerry Marsden** - Mrs Brown, You've Got A Lovely Daughter
The Bitter End Singers - Hard Times (I Got A Pretty Deaf Ear)
Medley: **The Everly Brothers** and **Gerry and The Pacemakers** perform each other's songs (last song features both): How Do You Do It? / Bye Bye Love / I Like It / Be-Bop-A-Lu La / Pretend (End of Medley)
Dick and Dee Dee - Some Things Just Stick In Your Mind
Gerry and The Pacemakers - It's Gonna Be Alright
Gary Lewis and The Playboys - Save Your Heart For Me
The Bitter End Singers - I Ain't Gonna Take It Sittin' Down
The Everly Brothers - Cathy's Clown
P.J. Proby - Let The Water Run Down
Gerry and The Pacemakers - You'll Never Walk Alone
The Everly Brothers - I'll Never Get Over You
P.J. Proby - Can Your Monkey Do The Dog?

THE EVERLY BROTHERS: 1957's 'Wake Up Little Susie' was a US No. 1 in Pop, C&W and R&B and No. 2 in the UK, 1960's 'Cathy's Clown' got to No. 1 in US Pop, R&B and in the UK, and their latest single 'I'll Never Get Over You' was a UK No. 35. Gerry Marsden accidently hits Don Everly in the face with his guitar during the fun medley.

GARY LEWIS AND THE PLAYBOYS: Gary Lewis (Gary Harold Lee Levitch, b. 1946 - drums and vocals), David Costell (b. 1944 - guitar), David Walker (b. 1943 - guitar), Allan Ramsay (b. 1943 - d. 1985 - bass) and John West (b. 1939 - keyboards and electric accordion). Pop group from California. 'Count Me In' and 'Save Your Heart For Me' both peaked at No. 2 in the US charts. This is the first of 2 'Shindig!' appearances.

P.J. PROBY: 'Hold Me' is another performance of his UK hit, and 'Let The Water Run Down' got to No. 19 in the UK.

GARY BRENTO WEIS: Pop singer and songwriter, of whom little more is known.

CLIFF BENNETT AND THE REBEL ROUSERS: Cliff Bennett (Clifford Bennett, b. 1940 - vocals). Other members include Dave Wendels (b. 1942 - guitar), Bobby Thomson (Robert Thomson, b. 1942 - bass), Mick Burt (Michael William Burt, b. 1938 - d. 2014 - drums), Roy Young (Roy Frederick Young, b. 1934 - d. 2018 - keyboards, vocals), Moss Groves (Maurice Groves, b. 1940 - saxophone) and Sid Phillips (Bernard Phillips, d. 2015 - saxophone). Rhythm 'n' Blues and Soul group from London.

THE BITTER END SINGERS: Nancy Priddy (Nancy Lee Priddy, b. 1941), Tina Bohlman, Vilma Vaccaro, Lefty Baker (Eustace Britchforth, b. 1939 - d. 1971), Norris O'Neill and Robert Hider (Robert Townsend Hider). Folk group from New York City. 'Hard Times (I Got A Pretty Deaf Ear)' and 'I Ain't Gonna Take It Sittin' Down' were released on singles.

DICK AND DEE DEE: Jagger-Richards' 'Some Things Just Stick In Your Mind' was also a single for UK singer Vashti.

GERRY AND THE PACEMAKERS: 'It's Gonna Be Alright' reached No. 23 in the US and No. 24 in the UK, and 'You'll Never Walk Alone' was a UK No. 1.

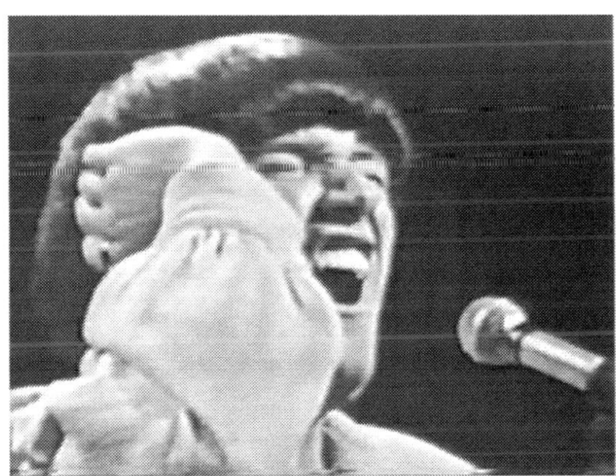

L-R: Petula Clark; Gary Lewis and The Playboys; P.J. Proby; Cliff Bennett and The Rebel Rousers; The Everly Brothers and Gerry and The Pacemakers; The Bitter End Singers

Episode 41: 23rd June 1965

Opening Medley: **Willy Nelson** with **David Crosby** and **Jim McGuinn** (of **The Byrds**) - Long Tall Sally / **The Righteous Brothers** - Sticks and Stones / **The Kingsmen** and **Billy Preston** - Good Golly Miss Molly (End of Medley)
The Byrds - Not Fade Away
Micki Lynn - Crazy 'Bout My Baby
The Stoneman Family - Lost Ball In The High Weeds
Melinda Marx - Is That What I Get For Loving You?
The Kingsmen - Louie, Louie
The Shindig Dancers - Hey Sport
Billy Preston - Hey! Hey! Hey! Hey!
Willy Nelson - Shout + Jump Back
Micki Lynn - The Old Landmark
Dave Berry - The Crying Game *
Adam Faith - A Message To Martha (Kentucky Bluebird) *
Jody Miller - Queen Of The House
The Righteous Brothers - Burn On Love
The Byrds - Mr. Tambourine Man
The Stoneman Family - Big Ball In Monterey
Dave Berry - One Heart Between Two *
The Righteous Brothers - Poison Ivy
Jody Miller - Saved
Jean King - Why Did I Choose You?
The Everly Brothers - I'll Never Get Over You
The Kingsmen - The Climb

MICKI LYNN: Jazz and Soul singer. Her cover of Robert Mosley's 'Crazy 'Bout My Baby' was a 1965 single.

THE STONEMAN FAMILY: Country and Folk group from Tennessee.

MELINDA MARX: Melinda Marie Marx (b. 1946). Pop singer and actress from Los Angeles, California. Groucho Marx's daughter, Melinda Marx released a couple of singles, but her fine version of The Ronettes' 'Is This What I Get For Loving You?' wasn't on any of them.

THE KINGSMEN: 'The Climb' got to No. 65, and 'Louie Louie' just missed the US top spot at No. 2

DAVE BERRY: 'The Crying Game' got to No. 5 in the UK and 'One Heart Between Two' peaked at No. 41.

ADAM FAITH: 'A Message To Martha (Kentucky Bluebird)' was a No. 12 hit in the UK.

JODY MILLER: An 'answer' record to Roger Miller's (no relation) 'King Of The Road', 'Queen Of The House' got to No. 12 on the US Pop charts and No. 5 in C&W.

THE BYRDS: Jim McGuinn (James Joseph McGuinn, b. 1942 - guitar and vocals), Gene Clark (Harold Eugene Clark, b. 1944 - d. 1991 - vocals, tambourine and guitar), David Crosby (David Van Cortlandt Crosby, b. 1941 - guitar and vocals), Chris Hillman (Christopher Hillman, b. 1944 - bass and vocals) and Michael Clarke (Michael James Dick, b. 1946 - d. 1993 - drums). Folk-Rock group from Los Angeles, California. 'Mr. Tambourine Man' topped the charts in both the US and UK. The band would make a further 2 'Shindig!' appearances.

THE EVERLY BROTHERS: 'I'll Never Get Over You' is another performance of their UK No. 35 hit.

L-R: David Crosby and Jim McGuinn (The Byrds); Micki Lynn; Melinda Marx; Dave Berry; Adam Faith; The Everly Brothers

Episode 42: 30th June 1965

Opening Medley: **Bobby Sherman** and **The Wellingtons** - At The Hop / **The Blossoms** and **Donna Loren** - (I Do The) Shimmy Shimmy / **Jackie Wilson** - Shake! Shake! Shake! / **Jerry Lee Lewis** - Jenny, Jenny (End of Medley)

Donna Loren - Rock Me In The Cradle Of Love

The Righteous Brothers - Tell The Truth

Bobby Sherman and **Donna Loren** - Casting My Spell

Chad and Jeremy - Before and After

The Shindig Dancers - South Street

The Shindogs - My Baby Left Me

Jackie Wilson - No Pity (In The Naked City)

Jerry Lee Lewis - Rocking Pneumonia and Boogie Woogie Flu

The Shindogs - A Hard Day's Night

Jackie Wilson - That's Why (I Love You So)

Glen Campbell - Cumberland Gap

The Shindogs and **Bobby Sherman** - Good Morning Little Schoolgirl

Bobby Hatfield - Hey Little Girl

Donna Loren - My Boyfriend's Back

Bill Medley - Charlie Brown

Jerry Lee Lewis - High School Confidential

The Blossoms - (He's Gonna Be) Fine, Fine, Fine

Chad and Jeremy - A Summer Song

Bobby Sherman - You Can't Sit Down

The Righteous Brothers and **The Blossoms** - Night Time Is The Right Time

Jackie Wilson - I'm So Lonely

Jerry Lee Lewis, **The Righteous Brothers** and **Jackie Wilson** - Whole Lotta Shakin' Going On

JACKIE WILSON: 1963's 'Shake! Shake! Shake!' was a US Pop No. 33 and R&B No. 21, 1959's 'That's Why (I Love You So)' a US Pop No. 13 and R&B No. 2, his latest record 'No Pity (In The Naked City)' a US Pop No. 59 and R&B No. 25, and 'I'm So Lonely' was the song's B-side.

CHAD AND JEREMY: 'Before and After' was a US No. 17 and 'A Summer Song' got to US No. 7.

JERRY LEE LEWIS: 'Rocking Pneumonia and Boogie Woogie Flu', performed on a harpsichord rather than a piano, was his latest non-charting single, 1958's 'High School Confidential' was a US Pop No. 21, C&W No. 9, R&B No. 5 and UK No. 12, and 'Whole Lotta Shakin' Going On' is yet another performance of his 1957 giant hit.

THE RIGHTEOUS BROTHERS AND THE BLOSSOMS: Even on a show with ultimate showmen Jerry Lee Lewis and Jackie Wilson, their performance of Ray Charles' 'Night Time Is The Right Time' is one of the highlights.

L-R; Donna Loren; Chad and Jeremy; Jackie Wilson; Jerry Lee Lewis, Glen Campbell; The Blossoms

Episode 43: 7th July 1965

Opening Medley: **Bobby Sherman**, **Donna Loren**, **The Eligibles** and **The Blossoms** - You Really Got Me / **Rick Lancelot** - All Day and All Of The Night / **The Kinks** - I'm A Lover Not A Fighter (End of Medley)
Sonny and Cher - It's Gonna Rain
Cher - Dream Baby
Billy Preston - (I Can't Get No) Satisfaction
The Gauchos - I Ain't Got You
Marianne Faithfull - Medley: What Have They Done To The Rain? / As Tears Go By
Bobby Sherman - Bring It On Home To Me
Rick Lancelot - Boom Boom
The Blossoms - Gimme Some
Donna Loren - Bad Boy
The Gauchos - I Like It Like That
Aretha Franklin - Shoop Shoop Song (It's In His Kiss)
Sonny Bono - My Girl Josephine
Marianne Faithfull - Come and Stay With Me
The Kinks - It's All Right
Donna Loren - Shakin' All Over
The Eligibles - A Little Bit Too Late
Aretha Franklin - (No, No) I'm Losing You
The Kinks - Set Me Free
Marianne Faithfull - This Little Bird
Bobby Sherman - I Saw Her Standing There
The Blossoms - Can't Believe What You Say (For Seeing What You Do)
The Kinks - Tired Of Waiting For You
Sonny and Cher - I Got You Babe
The Kinks - Long Tall Shorty

THE KINKS: 'Set Me Free' was a US No. 23 and UK No. 9, and 'Tired Of Waiting For You' a US No. 6 and UK No. 1. Their covers of Lazy Lester's 'I'm A Lover Not A Fighter' and Tommy Tucker's 'Long Tall Shorty' both feature Dave Davies on lead vocals.

MARIANNE FAITHFULL: 'What Have They Done To The Rain?' is a track from the UK and US 'Marianne Faithfull' albums, 'As Tears Go By' was a US No. 22 and UK No. 9, 'Come and Stay With Me' got to No. 26 in the US and No. 4 in the UK, and 'This Little Bird' reached No. 32 in the US and No. 6 in the UK.

DONNA LOREN: 'Bad Boy' is a Larry Williams song, revived in 1965 by The Beatles. Better still is her performance of Johnny Kidd and The Pirates' 'Shakin' All Over'.

ARETHA FRANKLIN: Her current single, '(No, No) I'm Losing You' peaked at No. 114 in the US Pop charts. 'Shoop Shoop Song (It's In His Kiss)' was first recorded by Merry Clayton though it was Betty Everett's cover that was more successful.

SONNY BONO: First recorded by Fats Domino as 'My Girl Josephine', the song is perhaps better known as 'Hello Josephine' thanks to Jerry Lee Lewis' cover.

SONNY AND CHER: 'I Got You Babe' topped the charts in both the US and UK.

L-R: Sonny and Cher; Billy Preston; Marianne Faithfull; Aretha Franklin; The Kinks; The Blossoms

Episode 44: 14th July 1965

Opening Medley: **Bobby Sherman** - Rave On / **The Beau Brummels**, **Kelly Garrett** and **Sammy Jackson** - Do You Wanna Dance? / **The Shindogs** - Fun, Fun, Fun (End of Medley)
Kelly Garrett - Boy On The Drums
Billy Preston - All About Melanie (Instrumental)
Ian Whitcomb - I'm Henry The VIII, I Am
The Gauchos - For You My Love
The Shindogs - I'm Talking About You
The Blossoms - Goodbye, So Long
Bobby Sherman - Catch The Wind
Sammy Jackson - Memphis
Terry Black - Unless You Care
The Gauchos - Seventh Son
George Wydell - Do The Walk
Shelley Fabares - My Prayer
Ian Whitcomb - N-E-R-V-O-U-S!
The Beau Brummels - Just A Little
The Wellingtons - Lotus 23 + Restless Rookie
Kelly Garrett - Fastest Little Racer
Bobby Sherman - My Ferrari GTO
The Beau Brummels - Sad Little Girl
The Shindogs - She's Fine, She's Mine
Bobby Sherman - For Your Love
Sammy Jackson - Hard Headed Woman
The Beau Brummels - You Tell Me Why
Ian Whitcomb - You Turn Me On (Turn On Song)

KELLY GARRETT: 'Boy On The Drums' was released as a single.

THE SHINDOGS: Surprisingly, The Shindogs' version of Chuck Berry's 'I'm Talking About You' copies The Hollies' arrangement rather than the original. 'She's Fine, She's Mine' is a Bo Diddley song that was covered by The Pretty Things.

SAMMY JACKSON: (b. 1937 - d. 1995). Rockabilly and Country singer from Henderson, North Carolina. Best remembered for his role in the TV series 'No Time For Sergeants', he does OK here.

TERRY BLACK: (b. 1949 - d. 2009). Pop singer from Vancouver, Canada. 'Unless You Care' stalled at No. 99 in the US but went all the way to No. 2 in his home country. This is the first of 2 'Shindig!' appearances.

GEORGE WYDELL: George Jones (b. 1936 - d. 2008). Soul singer from Richmond, Virginia. The former lead singer for Doo Wop group The Edsels, 'Do The Walk' was his first solo single.

SHELLEY FABARES: Michele Ann Marie Fabares (b. 1944). Pop singer and actress from Santa Monica, California. 'My Prayer' was a 1965 single for her.

IAN WHITCOMB: 'You Turn Me On (Turn On Song)' was a US No. 8 hit, and 'N-E-R-V-O-U-S!' a US No. 59 hit. Both were Rhythm 'n' Blues parodies rather than the real thing.

THE BEAU BRUMMELS: 'Just A Little' was a US No. 8 hit and 'You Tell Me Why' peaked at No. 38.

L-R: Ian Whitcomb; The Gauchos; Sammy Jackson, George Wydell; Shelley Fabares; The Beau Brummels

Episode 45: 21st July 1965

Opening Medley: **Gene Pitney** - Carol / **The Sir Douglas Quintet** - Roll Over Beethoven / **Bruce Scott** - Maybelline / **Sonny and Cher** - Ride On Josephine (End of Medley)
The Righteous Brothers - Justine
Gary Lewis and The Playboys - Save Your Heart For Me
Billy Preston - Do The Boomerang
The Nashville Teens - Tobacco Road *
Jody Miller - Silver Threads and Golden Needles
Billy Preston - Maggie's Farm
Gene Pitney - Looking Through The Eyes Of Love
Bobby Sherman - Seventh Son
Gary Lewis and The Playboys - Diamond Ring
Bruce Scott - Sweet Little Sixteen
The Chiffons - Nobody Knows What's Goin' On (In My Mind But Me)
The Sir Douglas Quintet - She's About A Mover
Bruce Scott - Let The Little Girl Dance
Sonny and Cher - Do You Love Me?
Gene Pitney - Last Chance To Turn Around
The Eligibles and **The Blossoms** - I Want Candy
The Righteous Brothers - In That Great Gettin' Up Morning
Cher - All I Really Want To Do
The Blossoms - I Can't Help Myself (Sugar Pie Honey Bunch)
The Sir Douglas Quintet - The Tracker
Gene Pitney - The Race Is On
The Righteous Brothers - Here 'Tis

SONNY AND CHER: Cher's superb solo performance of Bob Dylan's 'All I Really Want To Do' was a US No. 15 and UK No. 9 hit. 'Ride On Josephine' was originally by Bo Diddley, and 'Do You Love Me?' was by The Contours, topping the UK charts in a cover by Brian Poole and The Tremeloes.

GARY LEWIS AND THE PLAYBOYS: 'Save Your Heart For Me' is another performance of their US No. 2 hit, and 'This Diamond Ring' was a US chart topper.

THE NASHVILLE TEENS: Ray Phillips (Ramon John Philips, b. 1939 - vocals), Art Sharp (Arthur Sharp, b. 1941 - vocals), John Allen (John Samuel Allen, b. 1945 - guitar), Pete Shannon Harris (bass), John Hawken (John Christopher Hawken, b. 1940 - piano) and Barry Jenkins (Colin Ernest Jenkins, b. 1944 - drums). Rhythm 'n' Blues Group from Weybridge, Surrey, UK. 'Tobacco Road' was a US No. 14 and UK No. 6. This is the first of 2 consecutive 'Shindig!' appearances.

JODY MILLER: Her latest single, 'Silver Threads and Golden Needles' got to No. 54 in the US charts.

GENE PITNEY: His latest single, 'Looking Through The Eyes Of Love' was a US No. 28 and UK No. 3, and 'Last Chance To Turn Around' was a US No. 13. 'The Race Is On' is a song originally by Country singer George Jones, an artist whom Gene Pitney cut a couple of enjoyable duet albums with in 1965.

BRUCE SCOTT: Bruce Scott Zahariades (b. 1947). Actor and singer from New York City. This is the first of 2 'Shindig!' performances.

THE CHIFFONS: Judy Craig, Patricia Bennett, Barbara Lee and Sylvia Peterson. Girl group from The Bronx, New York City. 'Nobody Knows What's Goin' On (In My Mind But Me)' was a US No. 49 Pop hit.

THE SIR DOUGLAS QUINTET: Doug Sahm (Douglas Wayne Sahm, b. 1941 - d. 1999 - vocals, guitar), Jack Barber (bass), Johnny Perez (drums), Augie Meyers (August Meyers, b. 1940 - keyboards) and Frank Morin (saxophone and percussion). Rhythm 'n' Blues and Country-Rock band from San Antonio, California. 'She's About A Mover' reached No. 13 in the US charts and No. 15 in the UK, but the sound-alike follow-up 'The Tracker' failed to chart.

L-R: Gary Lewis and The Playboys; The Nashville Teens; Gene Pitney; The Chiffons; The Sir Douglas Quintet; The Righteous Brothers

Episode 46: 28th July 1965

Opening Medley: **Dave Clark** - Drum Solo (short) / **Jay and The Americans** - Do You Love Me? / **Donna Loren** - Shake, Rattle and Roll / **Terry Black** - Good Golly Miss Molly / **The Blossoms** - Hippy Hippy Shake / **Roy Clark** - Shake, Rattle and Roll / **Linda Carr** - Reelin' and Rockin' / **The Dave Clark Five** - Reelin' and Rockin' (End of Medley)
Tommy Tucker - Hi-Heel Sneakers
Jay and The Americans - This Land Is Your Land
Donna Loren - To Know Him Is To Love Him
Mike Clifford - New Orleans
Billy Preston - Too Much Monkey Business
Roy Clark - Twelfth Street Rag
Mike Clifford - Stay
The Wellingtons - Go Go Girls
Dave Berry - Memphis, Tennessee *
Linda Carr - Pain In My Heart
The Dave Clark Five - Glad All Over + Bits And Pieces
John Andrea - Route 66
Donna Loren - Long Live Love
Tommy Tucker - Just For A Day
The Dave Clark Five - Can't You See That She's Mine
Roy Clark - Sally Was A Good 'Ol Girl
Linda Carr - Tell Me What You're Gonna Do
Terry Black - Only Sixteen
The Blossoms - Can I Get A Witness
Tommy Tucker - Walking The Dog
Jay and The Americans - Cara Mia
The Nashville Teens - Google Eye *
The Dave Clark Five - I Like It Like That
Roy Clark with **The Dave Clark Five** - Bread and Butter Man

THE DAVE CLARK FIVE: 'Reelin' and Rockin'' was a US No. 23 and UK No. 24, 'Glad All Over' a US No. 6 and UK No. 1, 'Bits and Pieces' a US No. 4 and UK No. 2, 'Can't You See That She's Mine' a US No. 4 and UK No. 10, and 'I Like It Like That' a US No. 7. The finale with Roy Clark 'Bread and Butterman' was a Jerry Lee Lewis B-side from a year or so earlier, an odd choice as few would've known it.

TOMMY TUCKER: Robert Higginbotham (b. 1933 - d. 1982). Rhythm 'n' Blues singer and pianist from Springfield, Ohio. 'Hi-Heel Sneakers' reached No. 11 in the US Hot 100, as well as No. 23 in the UK.

JAY AND THE AMERICANS: Their latest single, 'Cara Mia' was a US No. 4 hit.

MIKE CLIFFORD: (b. 1943). Pop singer and songwriter from Los Angeles, California. This is the first of 2 'Shindig!' appearances.

DAVE BERRY: His first single from 1963, Chuck Berry's 'Memphis, Tennessee' got to No. 19 in the UK charts.

LINDA CARR: 'Tell Me What You're Gonna Do' is a great version of a James Brown song.

TERRY BLACK: His cover of Sam Cooke's 'Only Sixteen' failed to chart in the US but went to No. 14 in his native Canada.

THE NASHVILLE TEENS: Taped on the same day as their performance in Episode 45, 'Google Eye' was a US No. 117 and UK No. 10.

L-R: Tommy Tucker; Roy Clark; Dave Berry; Linda Carr; The Dave Clark Five; The Nashville Teens

Episode 47: 4th August 1965

Opening Medley: **Jerry Naylor** - You Turn Me On / **Billy Preston** - Seventh Son / **Jackie and Gayle** with **Bobby Sherman** - It Happened Just That Way / **The Righteous Brothers** - Burn On Love (End of Medley)
The Nooney Rickett 4 - Maybe The Last Time
Billy Preston - Clarabella
Marianne Faithfull - In My Time Of Sorrow *
Jerry Naylor - Early In The Morning
Bobby Sherman - Got My Mojo Working
The Righteous Brothers - Keep A Knockin'
Linda Clark - Oh Boy
Jackie and Gayle - When You Walk In The Room
The Great Scots - Rockin' Robin
Bobby Sherman - Wabash Cannonball
Bobby Hatfield - Unchained Melody
The Dixie Cups - I'm Gonna Get You Yet
The Nooney Rickett 4 - Shame, Shame, Shame
Linda Clark with **Jackie and Gayle** - Let The Sun Shine In
Billy Preston - (I'm Your) Hoochie Coochie Man
Terry Allen - Medley: Red Bird / Freedom School
The Great Scots - Give Some Lovin'
The Dixie Cups - Two-Way-Poc-A-Way
Jerry Naylor - City Lights
Marianne Faithfull - Paris Bells *
The Righteous Brothers - You Are My Sunshine
Linda Clark - Looking For My Pig
The Nooney Rickett 4 with **The Righteous Brothers** and **Jackie and Gayle** - Shout

THE NOONEY RICKETT 4: Rhythm 'n' Blues and Pop group from California. Their cover of James Brown's 'Maybe The Last Time' was released as a single.

BILLY PRESTON: First recorded by The Jodimars in 1956, 'Clarabella' was revived in 1963 by The Beatles for BBC radio.

MARIANNE FAITHFULL: 'In My Time Of Sorrow' and 'Paris Bells' are tracks from the US and UK 'Marianne Faithfull' albums.

BOBBY HATFIELD: Credited to The Righteous Brothers despite only featuring Bobby Hatfield, 'Unchained Melody' got to No. 4 in the USA and No. 14 in the UK (it would top the UK charts in 1990 after being featured in the movie 'Ghost').

TERRY ALLEN: (b. 1943). Country-Rock singer and songwriter from Wichita, Kansas. Here he manages to play piano and kazoo at the same time. He would find greater success in the '70s.

THE DIXIE CUPS: Their current single, 'Two-Way-Poc-A-Way' failed to chart.

THE GREAT SCOTS: Rick McNeil (vocals), Bill Schnare (guitar), Wayne Forrest (guitar), Dave Isnor (bass) and Gerry Archer (drums). Pop group from Nova Scotia, Canada. 'Give Me Lovin'' was their current single.

JERRY NAYLOR: 'City Lights' was his latest single.

LINDA CLARK: A singer for whom very little is known, 'Looking For My Pig' is a song written and originally recorded by Joe Tex.

L-R: The Nooney Rickett 4; Marianne Faithfull; The Great Scots, The Dixie Cups; Linda Clark; Terry Allen

Episode 48: 11th August 1965

Opening Medley: **Bobby Goldsboro** and **Donna Loren** - I Go Ape / **Joey Paige** - Move It / **The Shindogs** - Rock and Roll Music / **Glen Campbell** - Way Down Yonder In New Orleans / **The Blossoms** and **The Wellingtons** - Shake Rattle and Roll / **The Ronettes** - All Shook Up / **Sonny and Cher** - Yakety Yak / **Billy Preston** - Hound Dog / **The Righteous Brothers** - Justine (End of Medley)

The Shindogs - I Feel Fine

Glen Campbell - It Happened Just That Way

Joey Paige - I Just Want To Make Love To You

The Wellingtons - People Get Ready

Donna Loren - Sunshine, Lollipops, and Rainbows

The Ronettes - Be My Baby

Bobby Goldsboro - Voodoo Woman

Sonny and Cher - I Got You Babe

Billy Preston - Whole Lotta Shakin' Going On

Joey Paige - The Under Assistant West Coast Promotion Man

The Shindogs - Everybody's Trying To Be My Baby

Donovan - Catch The Wind

The Rolling Stones - Oh, Baby (We Got A Good Thing Going) *

The Righteous Brothers - Hung On You

Sonny Bono - Laugh At Me

Glen Campbell - What's New Pussycat?

Donna Loren - All My Loving

Donovan - Colours

Bobby Goldsboro - If You've Got A Heart

The Righteous Brothers - Turn On Your Love Light

The Ronettes - Born To Be Together

The Rolling Stones - Down The Road A Piece *

The Righteous Brothers - This Little Girl Of Mine

JOEY PAIGE: Joseph E. Sauseris. Pop and Rhythm 'n' Blues singer from Philadelphia. Muddy Waters' 'I Just Want To Make Love To You' is based on The Rolling Stones version, while 'The Under Assistant West Coast Promotion Man' is a song written and recorded by The Rolling Stones.

THE RONETTES: Ronnie Bennett (Veronica Yvette Bennett, b. 1943), Estelle Bennett (b. 1941 - d. 2009) and Nedra Talley (b. 1946). Girl Group from New York City. 'Born To Be Together' peaked at No. 52 in the US charts, while 'Be My Baby' was the group's biggest hit, getting to No. 2 in the US and No. 4 in the UK.

BOBBY GOLDSBORO: 'Voodoo Woman' was a US No. 27 hit, and 'If You've Got A Heart' got to No. 60.

SONNY AND CHER: 'I Got You Babe' is a 2nd performance of their US and UK No. 1, and Sonny's solo 'Laugh At Me' was a US No. 10 hit.

BILLY PRESTON: 'Whole Lotta Shakin' Going On' closely follows his old boss Little Richard's version.

DONOVAN: Donovan Phillips Leitch (b. 1946). Folk and Pop singer and guitarist from Glasgow, Scotland, UK. 'Catch The Wind' was a US No. 23 and 'Colours' a US No. 61 in the US, while both songs peaked at No. 4 in the UK. This is the first of 2 'Shindig!' appearances.

THE ROLLING STONES: 'Oh, Baby (We Got A Good Thing Going)' and 'Down The Road Apiece' are both from the US 'The Rolling Stones, Now!' album, with the former also on the UK version of 'Out Of Our Heads' and the latter on the UK 'The Rolling Stones No. 2'. The performance was taped in London on 12th December 1964.

L-R: Joey Paige; The Ronettes; Sonny and Cher; Donovan; The Rolling Stones; Bobby Goldsboro

Episode 49: 18th August 1965

Opening Medley: **The Shindogs** - Ride On Josephine / **Bobby Sherman** - Pretty Thing / **Jay P. Moby** - Bo Diddley / **Eddie Hodges**, **Glen Campbell** and **Bo Diddley** - Mama Don't Allow No Twistin' (End of Medley)
Tina Turner - I Don't Need
The Shindogs - Dizzy Miss Lizzy
Glen Campbell - Don't You Rock Me, Daddy-O
Patty Michaels - Mrs Johnny
Eddie Hodges - New Orleans
Billy Preston - (I Can't Get No) Satisfaction
Tina Turner with **The Blossoms** - Good Bye, So Long
Jay P. Moby - Don't Cry No More
Jackie DeShannon - What The World Needs Now Is Love
Bo Diddley - Give Me A Break + You Can't Judge A Book By The Cover
Dick and Dee Dee - Thou Shalt Not Steal
Eddie Rambeau - Concrete and Clay
Bo Diddley - Road Runner
Tina Turner with **The Blossoms** - I Can't Believe What You Say (For Seeing What You Do)
Bobby Sherman - Down In The Boondocks
The Shindogs - It's All Over Now
Fanita James (of **The Blossoms**) - Hush Hush, Sweet Charlotte
Glen Campbell - Rip It Up
Medley: **Bobby Sherman** - On The Beach / **Jay P. Moby**, **Eddie Rambeau** and **Dick St James** - Surf City / **The Wellingtons** and **Eddie Hodges** - Noble Surfer / **Patty Michaels**, **Dee Dee** and **Jackie DeShannon** - Surfin' USA / **The Wellingtons** - The Girls On The Beach / **Bobby Sherman** - On The Beach (Reprise)
Eddie Rambeau - My Name Is Mud
Dick and Dee Dee - Don't Think Twice, It's Alright
Jackie DeShannon - Feel So Fine
Bo Diddley - Hey! Bo Diddley
Jay P. Moby, **Bo Diddley** and **Tina Turner** - Can Your Monkey Do The Dog?

JAY P. MOBY: Rubén Funkahuatl Ladrón de Guevara (b. 1942). Rhythm 'n' Blues and Soul singer from Los Angeles, California.

TINA TURNER: All 3 songs Ike and Tina Turner's singles, 'I Don't Need' was a US Pop No. 134, 'Good Bye, So Long' a US Pop No. 107 and R&B No. 32, and 'I Can't Believe What You Say (For Seeing What You Do)' a US Pop No. 95.

PATTY MICHAELS: (b. 1950). Singer and actress from Queens, New York. 'Mrs. Johnny' was released as a non-charting single.

EDDIE HODGES: Samuel Hodges (b. 1947). Singer and actor from Hattiesburg, Mississippi.

JACKIE DESHANNON: A 2nd 'Shindig!' performance of her No. 7 hit 'What The World Needs Now Is Love'.

BO DIDDLEY: Ellas Otha Bates, later changed to Ellas McDaniel (b. 1928 - d. 2008). Rock 'n' Roll and Rhythm 'n' Blues singer and guitarist from McComb, Mississippi. 'You Can't Judge A Book By The Cover' was No. 48 US Pop Hit and No. 21 R&B in 1962, and 1960's 'Road Runner' peaked at No. 75 Pop and No. 20 R&B.

DICK AND DEE DEE: Yet another performance of their No. 13 US hit 'Thou Shalt Not Steal'.

EDDIE RAMBEAU: Edward Cletus Fluri (b. 1943). Pop singer and actor from Hazleton, Pennsylvania. 'Concrete and Clay' was a US No. 35 hit, and 'My Name Is Mud' a US No.112. This is the first of 2 'Shindig!' appearances.

L-R: Patty Michaels; Jay P. Moby; Jackie DeShannon; Bo Diddley; Tina Turner; Dick and Dee Dee

Episode 50: 1st September 1965 (some sources list this as 25th August 1965)

Opening Medley: **Bobby Sherman** - Susie Q / **The Shindogs** - I'm A Fool / **Glen Campbell** - Hard Headed Woman / **Kathy Kersh** - Evil (End of Medley)
The Off-Beats - Mary
Kathy Kersh - You'd Better Come Home
Booker T. and The M.G.'s - Boot-Leg
Bobby Sherman - Lover Please
Glen Campbell - The Wrong Yo Yo
Billy Preston - Shake and Fingerpop
The Shindogs and **The Eligibles** - Help!
Jean-Paul Vignon - What Now My Love?
Glen Campbell - Hallelujah I Love Her So
Cathie Taylor - Rock Me In The Cradle Of Love
James Brown - Papa's Got A Brand New Bag
Glen Campbell - I'm Alive
Bobby Sherman - Heart Full Of Soul
The Shindogs - The Price Of Love
The Off-Beats - It's Alright
Bobby Sherman - Wooly Bully
The Kinks - I'm A Lover Not A Fighter *
Booker T. and The M.G.'s - Big Train + Green Onions
Cathie Taylor - A-Round The Corner
The Off-Beats - You Know I Need You
James Brown - Please, Please, Please
Jean-Paul Vignon - It's My Party
Kathy Kersh and **Bobby Sherman** - You Can't Sit Down
The Kinks - Beautiful Delilah *
James Brown - Night Train

KATHY KERSH: Kathleen Kroeger Kersh (b. 1942). Actress and singer from Los Angeles, California.

THE OFF-BEATS: Pop and Garage group from California. 'Mary' was the A-side of their only single. 'It's Alright' is a Bo Diddley song covered by The Rolling Stones.

BOOKER T. AND THE M.G.'S: Booker Taliaferro Jones Jr. (b. 1944 - keyboards), Steve Cropper (Steven Lee Cropper, b. 1941 - guitar), Donald 'Duck' Dunn (Donald Dunn, b. 1941 - d. 2012 - bass) and Al Jackson Jr. (Albert J. Jackson Jr., b. 1935 - d. 1975 - drums). Rhythm 'n' Blues and Soul instrumental group from Memphis, Tennessee. Their latest single, 'Boot-Leg' was a US No. 58 Pop and No. 10 R&B hit, while 1962's 'Green Onions' got to No. 3 in the Pop charts and No. 1 in R&B.

JEAN-PAUL VIGNON: (b. 1935). Pop singer and actor from France. 'What Now My Love' was released as a single. Lesley Gore's 'It's My Party' is performed in French.

CATHIE TAYLOR: (b. 1944). Canadian-born Country and Folk singer from California. 'A-Round The Corner' is a track from her album 'Cathie Taylor Sings Of The Land and The People'.

JAMES BROWN: James Joseph Brown (b. 1933 - d. 2006). Rhythm 'n' Blues and Soul singer from Augusta, Georgia. His latest single, 'Papa's Got A Brand New Bag' got to No. 8 in the US Pop charts and No. 1 in R&B, 'Please, Please, Please' was his debut single in 1956 which reached No. 6 R&B, and 1962's 'Night Train' was a No. 35 in Pop and No. 5 R&B.

THE KINKS: The performances on this show were taped in London on 17th December 1964. Both songs feature Dave Davies on lead vocals.

L-R: Kathy Kersh; The Kinks; Cathie Taylor; James Brown; Booker T. and The M.G.'s; Glen Campbell

Episode 51: 8th September 1965

Opening Medley: **Bruce Scott** - Baby Workout / **Barbara Lewis** - He's A Real Gone Guy / **Gene Chandler** - I Got A Woman / **The Blossoms** and **The Eligibles** - Rider / **The Collins Kids**, **Bruce Scott** and **John Andrea** - Don't Think Twice, It's Alright / **The Searchers** and **The Guilloteens** - I Got My Mojo Working (End of Medley)
Billy Preston - Agent Double-O-Soul
The Guilloteens - I Don't Believe
John Andrea and **The Eligibles** - Bread and Butter
Gene Chandler - (Gonna Be) Good Times
The Collins Kids - Like A Rolling Stone
The Eligibles - A Summer Place
Bruce Scott - Summertime Blues
Barbara Lewis - It's Not Unusual
The Searchers - He's Got No Love
Patty Duke - Say Something Funny
John Andrea and **The Eligibles** - California Girls
The Collins Kids - Ticket To Ride
The Blossoms - Saved
Barbara Lewis - Baby I'm Yours
The Zombies - She's Not There *
Patty Duke - Funny Little Butterflies
Medley: **Barbara Lewis** - Watermelon Man / **Gene Chandler** - Sugar Dumpling / **The Shindig Band** - Yakety Axe / **The Collins Kids** - Sunshine, Lollipops and Rainbows
Bruce Scott - Save Your Heart For Me
The Searchers - Love Potion No. 9 + Bumble Bee
Gene Chandler - Can I Get A Witness?

THE GUILLOTEENS: Laddie Hutcherson (vocals and guitar), Louis Paul (Louis Elmo Paul Jr., b. 1947 - 2015 - vocals and bass) and Joe Davis (Joe W. Davis III, b. 1945 - d. 2008 - drums). Garage band from Memphis, Tennessee. 'I Don't Believe' was their latest single (The Searchers learnt the song by also appearing on the show, and would eventually perform the song for BBC radio).

GENE CHANDLER: Eugene Drake Dixon (b. 1937). Pop and soul singer from Chicago, Illinois. '(Gonna Be) Good Times' was a US No. 92 Pop hit and No. 40 R&B.

THE COLLINS KIDS: Better remembered for their earlier Rockabilly performances and records, the duo both look and sound very contemporary here.

THE SEARCHERS: Mike Pender (Michael John Prendergast, b. 1941 - guitar and vocals), John McNally (b. 1941 - guitar and vocals), Frank Allen (Francis Renaud McNeice, b. 1943 - bass and vocals) and Chris Curtis (born Christopher Crummey, b. 1941 - d. 2005 - drums and vocals). Beat group from Liverpool. Their latest single, 'He's Got No Love' got to No. 79 in the US and No. 12 in the UK, 'Love Potion No. 9' was their biggest US hit at No. 3, while 'Bumble Bee' was a US No. 21 (the latter 2 songs were not released as singles in the UK). This is the first of 3 'Shindig!' appearances.

PATTY DUKE: 'Say Something Funny' got to No. 22 in the US charts.

THE ZOMBIES: 'She's Not There' was a US No. 1 and UK No. 12.

BARBARA LEWIS: Barbara Ann Lewis (b. 1943). Rhythm 'n' Blues and Soul singer from Salem, Michigan. 'Baby I'm Yours' was a US No. 11 hit. 'It's Not Unusual' is the Tom Jones song, and works surprisingly well here. This is the first of 2 'Shindig!' appearances.

L-R: Gene Chandler; The Searchers; Patty Duke; The Collins Kids; Barbara Lewis; The Zombies

Episode 52: 16th September 1965

Opening Medley: **The McCoys** and **The Byrds** - California Sun / **Jerry Naylor** - I Got A Feeling / **The Everly Brothers** - Rip It Up / **Chad and Jill** - Ready Teddy (End of Medley)

The Everly Brothers - Love Is Strange

The Byrds - I'll Feel A Whole Lot Better

Billy Preston - Short Fat Fanny

Jerry Naylor - Action

Ketty Lester - I'll Be Looking Back

The Byrds - The Bells Of Rhymney

The McCoys - Hang On Sloopy

Chad and Jill - I Don't Want To Lose You Baby

Chad Stuart - Funny How Love Can Be

The Rolling Stones - (I Can't Get No) Satisfaction

Everly Brothers - The Girl Can't Help It

THE EVERLY BROTHERS: 'Rip It Up' is a song from their 1957 debut album, 'Love Is Strange' was their current US No. 128 and UK No. 11 single, and Little Richard's 'The Girl Can't Help It' is a track from their latest album 'Beat & Soul'.

THE BYRDS: 'I'll Feel A Whole Lot Better' was the B-side of the US No. 40 and UK No. 4 'All I Really Want To Do' single, while 'The Bells Of Rhymney' is from their debut album 'Mr. Tambourine Man'.

BILLY PRESTON: 'Short Fat Fanny' was originally by Larry Williams (his biggest US hit, despite other songs being better known today).

KETTY LESTER: Her latest record, 'I'll Be Looking Back' didn't chart.

THE McCOYS: Rick Derringer (Richard Zehringer, b. 1947 - guitar and vocals), Randy Hobbs (Randy Jo Hobbs, b. 1948 - d. 1993 - bass and vocals), Bobbie Peterson (Robert Peterson, b. 1946 - d. 1993 - keyboards and vocals) and Randy Z (Randy Zehringer, b. 1949 - drums). Pop and rock band from Union City, Indiana. Originally recorded by The Vibrations as 'My Girl Sloopy', 'Hang On Sloopy' topped the US charts and reached No. 5 in the UK.

CHAD AND JILL: Chad Stuart of Chad and Jeremy fame, and his wife Jill Stuart (formerly Jill Gibson). Pop and Folk duo from UK. 'Funny How Love Can Be' was a top 10 UK hit for The Ivy League.

THE ROLLING STONES: Taped in the UK on 28th July 1965, this is a 2nd performance of The Rolling Stones' US/UK chart-topper, a song that got its world premiere on 'Shindig!' 4 months earlier. The line "Trying to make some girl" is censored.

L-R: The Byrds; Billy Preston; Ketty Lester; Chad and Jill; The Rolling Stones; The Everly Brothers

Episode 53: 18th September 1965

Opening Medley: **The Righteous Brothers** - Money Honey / **The Shindogs** and **The Wellingtons** - Two Hound Dogs / **Bobby Sherman** - Out Of Sight / **James Burton** - Instrumental / **Jackie DeShannon** - All Around The World (End of Medley)

The Dave Clark Five - Catch Us If You Can

Bobby Sherman, **The Wellingtons** and **The Blossoms** - Ju Ju Hand

The Shindogs and **The Wellingtons** - I'm Down

Marianne Faithfull - Summer Nights

The Righteous Brothers - Ko Ko Joe

Billy Preston - In The Midnight Hour

We Five - You Were On My Mind

Jackie DeShannon - Shop Around

Freddie and The Dreamers - Little Bitty Pretty One *

Jackie De Shannon, **Bobby Sherman**, **Delaney Bramlett** and **Joey Cooper** - Shake and Fingerpop

The Righteous Brothers - Medley: My Babe / Try To Find Another Man / Little Latin Lupe Lu / Ko Ko Joe

THE DAVE CLARK FIVE: The UK title track of their current movie, 'Catch Us If You Can' reached No. 4 in the US and No. 5 in the UK. In the USA the movie was instead called 'Having A Wild Weekend'.

BOBBY SHERMAN: 'Ju Ju Hand' was a single for Sam The Sham & The Pharaohs.

MARIANNE FAITHFULL: 'Summer Nights' reached No. 24 in the US and No. 10 in the UK.

WE FIVE: Beverly Bivens (b. 1946 - vocals), Michael Stewart (b. 1945 - d. 2002 - vocals and guitar), Jerry Burgan (b. 1945 - d. 2021 - vocals and guitar), Bob Jones (b. 1947 - d. 2013 - vocals and guitar) and Pete Fullerton (vocals and bass). Folk and Pop group from San Francisco, California. 'You Were On My Mind' was a US No. 3 hit. This is the first of 2 'Shindig!' appearances.

JACKIE DESHANNON: 'Shop Around' was a 1960 hit for The Miracles.

L-R: The Dave Clark Five; Marianne Faithfull; We Five; Jackie DeShannon; Freddie and The Dreamers; The Righteous Brothers

Episode 54: 23rd September 1965

Opening Medley: **Jerry Lee Lewis** - Breathless / **The Blossoms** - Johnny B. Goode / **The Wellingtons** - Whole Lotta Lovin' / **Billy Preston** - Baby, Please Don't Go (End of Medley)

Jerry Lee Lewis - High Heeled Sneakers

Mike Clifford with **The Wellingtons** - Ruby Baby

Raquel Welch with **The Blossoms** - Dancing In The Street

The Yardbirds - For Your Love *

Billy Preston and **The Blossoms** - Look At Me

Mike Clifford and **The Wellingtons** - Wonderful World

Jerry Lee Lewis - Mean Woman Blues

The Pretty Things - Honey, I Need *

The Blossoms - Nowhere To Run

The Yardbirds - Heart Full Of Soul *

Jerry Lee Lewis - Medley: High School Confidential / Great Balls Of Fire / Whole Lotta Shakin' Going On

JERRY LEE LEWIS: A live recording of 'Hi Heel Sneakers' was a US No. 91 hit in 1964. An EP track in the USA, 'Mean Woman Blues' was the 1957 B-side of his chart-topping 'Great Balls Of Fire' in the UK.

RAQUEL WELCH: Jo Raquel Tejada (b. 1940). Actress and occasional singer from Chicago, Illinois. She looks far more impressive than she sounds on 'Dancing In The Street'.

THE YARDBIRDS: Keith Relf (William Keith Relf, b. 1943 - d. 1976 - vocals and harmonica), Jeff Beck (Geoffrey Arnold Beck, b. 1944 - guitar and vocals), Chris Dreja (Christopher Walenty Dreja, b. 1945 - guitar), Paul Samwell-Smith (Paul Granville Samwell-Smith, b. 1943 - bass) and Jim McCarty (James Stanley McCarty, b. 1943 - drums and vocals). Rhythm 'n' Blues group from London. 'For Your Love' was a US No. 6 and UK No. 3, and 'Heart Full Of Soul' a US No. 9 and UK No. 2. This is the first of 4 'Shindig!' appearances.

MIKE CLIFFORD: 'Wonderful World' was a top 10 hit for Sam Cooke in 1960 and for Herman's Hermits in 1965.

THE PRETTY THINGS: Phil May (Philip Dennis Arthur Wadey, b. 1944 - d. 2020 - vocals), Dick Taylor (Richard Clifford Taylor, b. 1943 - guitar), Brian Pendleton (b. 1944 - d. 2001 - guitar and vocals), John Stax (Edward Lee Fullagar, b. 1944 - bass and vocals) and Viv Prince (Vivian Martin Prince, b. 1941 - drums). Rhythm 'n' Blues group from London. 'Honey I Need' was a UK No. 13 hit. This is the first of 2 'Shindig!' appearances.

L-R: Jerry Lee Lewis; Mike Clifford; Raquel Welch; The Yardbirds; The Blossoms, The Pretty Things

Episode 55: 28th September 1965

Opening Medley: **Dick and Dee Dee** - Sha La La / **Jimmie Rodgers** - Early In The Morning / **Donna Loren** - I Only Want To Be With You / **Little Anthony and The Imperials** - Can I Get A Witness? (End of Medley)

Mary Wells - Me Without You

Bobby Sherman - Mountain Of Love

Little Anthony and The Imperials - Hurt So Bad

Dick and Dee Dee - Vini Vini

Donna Loren - You've Got Your Troubles

Jimmie Rodgers - The World I Used To Know

Mary Wells - My Guy

Georgie Fame and The Blue Flames - Like We Used To Be *

Little Anthony and The Imperials - I Miss You So

Dick and Dee Dee - Liar, Liar

Bobby Sherman, **Donna Loren** and **Jimmie Rodgers** - Rock and Roll Music

Little Anthony and **The Imperials** - Good Lovin'

MARY WELLS: Her latest record, 'Me Without You' was a US No. 95 hit, and 'My Guy' is another performance of her US chart-topper.

LITTLE ANTHONY AND THE IMPERIALS: 'Hurt So Bad' is another performance of their US No. 10 hit, while their latest record 'I Miss You So' peaked at US Pop No. 34 and R&B No. 23.

DONNA LOREN: 'You've Got Your Troubles' was a Trans-Atlantic top 10 hit for The Fortunes, and as nearly always, Donna Loren handles the song with apparent ease.

JIMMIE RODGERS: 'The World I Used To Know' was a US No. 51 hit.

GEORGIE FAME AND THE BLUE FLAMES: Clive Powell (b. 1943). Rhythm 'n' Blues and Jazz singer, pianist and organist from Leigh, Lancashire, UK. The Blue Flames was his backing band until 1966. His current single, 'Like We Used To Be' was a UK No. 33. This is the first of 4 'Shindig!' appearances.

DICK AND DEE DEE: An unusual choice of song for Dick and Dee, 'Liar, Liar' was a US hit for The Castaways.

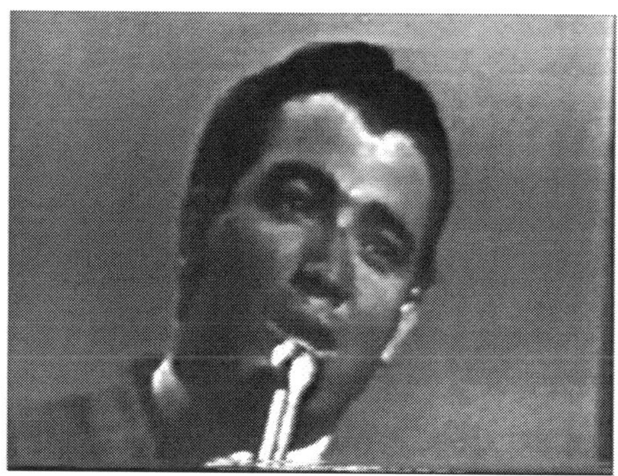

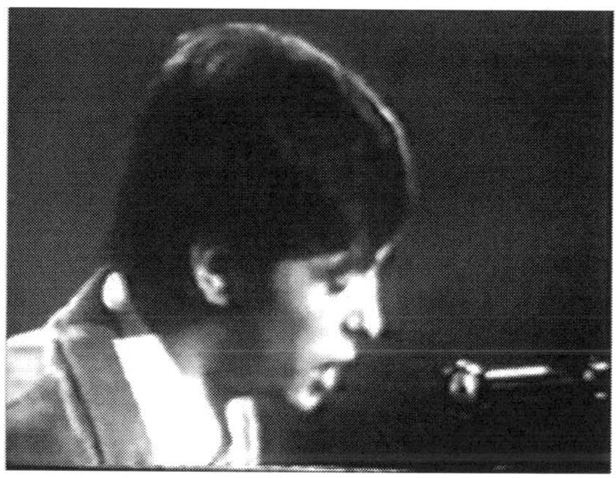

L-R: Mary Wells; Little Anthony and The Imperials; Dick and Dee Dee; Donna Loren; Jimmie Rodgers; Georgie Fame and The Blue Flames

Episode 56: 30 September 1965

Opening Medley: **The Turtles** - We'll Meet Again / **Lesley Gore** - It's My Party / **Major Lance** - Don't Set Me Free **/ The Blossoms** and **The Wellingtons** - Oh Boy / **Delaney Bramlett** and **Joey Cooper** - Dixieland Rock (End of Medley)

Major Lance - Too Hot To Hold

The Hollies - I'm Alive *

The Turtles - Needles and Pins

Lesley Gore - Judy's Turn To Cry

Donovan - Colours

Lesley Gore - My Town, My Guy and Me

The Shindogs - Act Naturally

Major Lance - Um, Um, Um, Um, Um, Um + The Monkey Time

The Searchers - Hi-Heel Sneakers *

The Turtles - It Ain't Me Babe

Lesley Gore - Sunshine, Lollipops and Rainbows

Major Lance - Land Of A Thousand Dances

LESLEY GORE: 'It's My Party' was a US No. 1 and UK No. 9, 'Judy's Turn To Cry' a US No. 5, her latest single 'My Town, My Guy and Me' a US No. 32, and 'Sunshine, Lollipops and Rainbows' a US No. 13.

THE HOLLIES: Allan Clarke (Harold Allan Clarke, b. 1942 - vocals and harmonica), Graham Nash (Graham William Nash, b. 1942 - vocals and guitar), Tony Hicks (Anthony Christopher Hicks, b. 1945 - guitar and vocals), Eric Haydock (Eric John Haddock, b. 1943 - d. 2019 - bass) and Bobby Elliott (Robert Hartley Elliott, b. 1941 - drums). Beat Group from Manchester, UK. 'I'm Alive' stalled at No. 103 in the US but topped the charts in the UK. This is the first of 3 'Shindig!' appearances, all of them taped in the UK on 30th July 1965, and all of them showing what a great live band they were.

DONOVAN: Another performance of his US No. 61 and UK No. 4 hit.

MAJOR LANCE: (b. 1939 - d. 1994). 'Um, Um, Um, Um, Um, Um' was a US Pop No. 5, R&B No. 1 and UK No. 40, and 'The Monkey Time' is another performance of his US Pop No. 8 and R&B No. 2.

THE SEARCHERS: The B-side of their big US hit 'Love Potion No. 9', Tommy Tucker's 'Hi-Heel Sneakers' is one of the few songs by the group to feature John McNally on lead vocals.

THE TURTLES: Howard Kaylan (b. 1947 - vocals), Mark Volman (b. 1947 - vocals and guitar), Al Nichol (guitar, keyboards and vocals), Jim Tucker (d. 2020 - guitar and vocals), Chuck Portz (bass) and Don Murray (Donald Ray Murray, b. 1945 - d. 1996 - drums). Folk-Rock and Pop group from Los Angeles, California. Bob Dylan's 'It Ain't Me Babe' was a US No. 8 hit. This is the first of 2 'Shindig!' appearances.

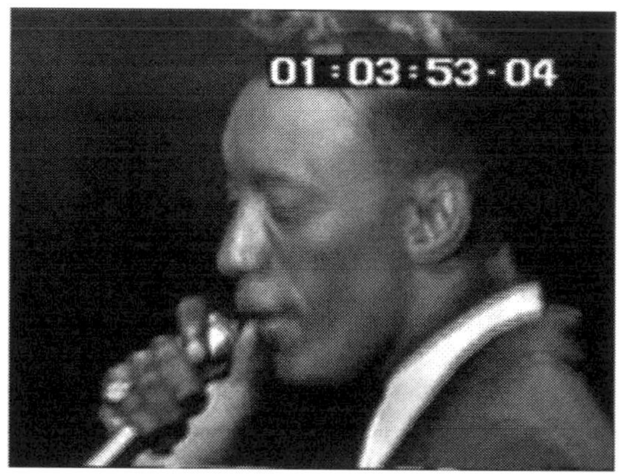

L-R: Major Lance; The Hollies; The Turtles; Lesley Gore; Donovan; The Searchers

Episode 57: 2nd October 1965

Opening Medley: **Ray Peterson** - Party / **Linda Gayle** - Do You Wanna Dance? / **The Four Tops** - Down The Road Apiece (End of Medley)
Billy Joe Royal - Down In The Boondocks
Linda Gayle - Home Of The Brave
The Four Tops - It's The Same Old Song
Ray Peterson - Mean Woman Blues
The Who - I Can't Explain *
The Blossoms - Lover's Concerto
Linda Gayle - Stop, Look, Listen
Billy Joe Royal - I Knew You When
Gerry and The Pacemakers - Ferry Cross The Mersey *
Ray Peterson - Let The Four Winds Blow
Ray Peterson - Mickey's Monkey

BILLY JOE ROYAL: (b. 1942 - d. 2015). Pop and Country singer from Valdosta, Georgia. 'Down In The Boondocks' was a US No. 9 hit and 'I Knew You When' was a US No. 14 hit. This is the first of 2 'Shindig!' performances.

LINDA GAYLE: Soul and Pop singer. Not to be confused with Jerry Lee Lewis' sister Linda Gail Lewis, 'Stop, Look, Listen' was a 1965 single, and 'Home Of The Brave' was a hit for Jody Miller.

THE FOUR TOPS: Their current single, 'It's The Same Old Song' was a US Pop No. 5, R&B No. 2 and UK No. 34.

THE WHO: Roger Daltrey (Roger Harry Daltrey, b. 1944 - vocals and harmonica), Pete Townshend (Peter Dennis Blandford Townshend, b. 1945 - guitar and vocals), John Entwistle (John Alec Entwistle (b. 1944 - d. 2002 - bass and vocals) and Keith Moon (Keith John Moon, b. 1946 - d. 1978 - drums and vocals). Rhythm 'n' Blues group from London, UK. Seen here in a performance taped in London on 3rd August 1965, 'I Can't Explain' got to No. 93 in the US and No. 8 in the UK. This is the first of 4 'Shindig!' performances.

GERRY AND THE PACEMAKERS: The title track to their movie, 'Ferry Cross The Mersey' was a US No. 6 and UK No. 8.

RAY PETERSON: 'Let The Four Winds Blow' was a 1961 single for Fats Domino.

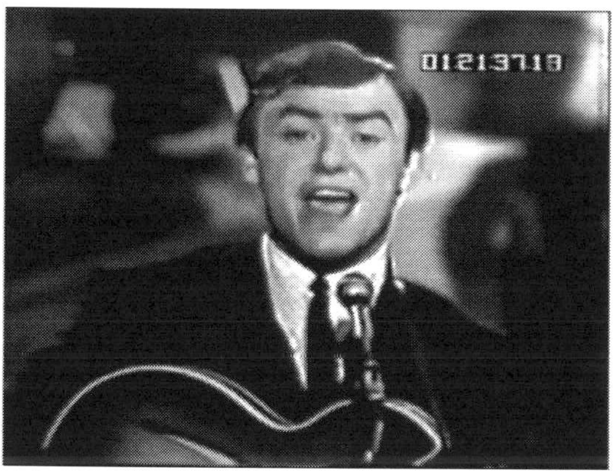

L-R: Billy Joe Royal; Linda Gayle; The Four Tops; The Who; Gerry and The Pacemakers; Ray Peterson

Episode 58: 7th October 1965

Opening Medley: **Evie Sands** - Live It Up / **Bobby Sherman** - You Must Have Been A Beautiful Baby / **Dee Dee Sharp** - Rock Me In The Cradle Of Love / **The Shindogs** - Come On Let's Go (End of Medley)

The Kinks - Who'll Be The Next In Line *

Evie Sands - Take Me For A Little While

Charlie Rich - Mohair Sam

Dee Dee Sharp - Do The Bird

Bobby Sherman with **The Wellingtons** - You're The One

Jean King - Something Happens To Me

Charlie Rich - Lonely Weekends

The Shindogs - The Night Before

The Kinks - See My Friends *

Dee Dee Sharp with **The Blossoms** - Mashed Potato Time

Billy Preston and **Dee Dee Sharp** - Slow Twistin'

Bobby Sherman and **Evie Sands** - Shu Rah

The Shindogs, **Dee Dee Sharp**, **Billy Preston** and **Bobby Sherman** - I'm Movin' On

DEE DEE SHARP: 'Rock Me In The Cradle Of Love' is another performance of her 1963 No. 43 hit, the same year's 'Do The Bird' was a US Pop No. 10 and R&B No. 8, 1962's 'Mashed Potato Time' a US Pop No. 2 and R&B No. 1, and 'Slow Twistin' (in a 1962 duet with Chubby Checker) a US Pop and R&B No. 3.

THE KINKS: 'Who'll Be The Next In Line' was a US No. 34, and 'See My Friends' a UK No. 10. The performances were taped in London on 4th August 1965.

EVIE SANDS: (b. 1946). Pop and soul singer from Brooklyn, New York. 'Take Me For A Little While' was a minor US hit, peaking at No. 114 in the US charts.

CHARLIE RICH: Charles Allan Rich (b. 1932 - d. 1995). Rock 'n' Roll, Country and Pop singer and pianist from Colt, Arkansas. 'Mohair Sam' was a US No. 21 hit, and 1960's 'Lonely Weekends' a US No. 22. The latter song is performed here away from the piano.

THE SHINDOGS: The 'Shindig!' house band often had great fun when performing songs by The Beatles, as they clearly do with 'The Night Before', even though the singer sounds more like Lennon than McCartney.

BOBBY SHERMAN AND EVIE SANDS: 'Shindig!' often featured Fats Domino songs, despite the non-appearance of the great man himself. 'Shu Rah' was a 1961 single.

L-R: The Kinks; Evie Sands; Charlie Rich; Dee Dee Sharp; Bobby Sherman with The Wellingtons; Jean King

Episode 59: 9th October 1965

Opening Medley: **Dick and Dee Dee** - Thou Shalt Not Steal / **Junior Walker** - You're A Wonderful One / **Jackie DeShannon** - It's Love Baby / **Roy Head** - You Can't Sit Down (End of Medley)
Dick and Dee Dee with **The Wellingtons** - I Live For The Sun
Jackie DeShannon - A Lifetime Of Loneliness
Junior Walker and **The All Stars** - Shotgun
Roy Head - Turn On Your Love Light
The Shindogs - Not The Lovin' Kind
Dick and Dee Dee - Roll Over Beethoven
Glen Campbell - Universal Soldier
Carolyn Jones (Guest Host) - This Little Bird
Junior Walker and The All Stars - Shake and Fingerpop
Jackie DeShannon with **The Blossoms** and **The Wellingtons** - I Go Crazy
Roy Head - Treat Her Right
Junior Walker and The All Stars - Shout

DICK AND DEE DEE: This is the 4th 'Shindig!' performance of their No. 13 hit 'Thou Shalt Not Steal'. 'I Live For The Sun' was originally by The Sunrays, and later a UK hit for Vanity Fare.

JACKIE DESHANNON: Jackie DeShannon's current single, 'A Lifetime Of Loneliness' peaked at No. 66 on the US charts.

JUNIOR WALKER AND THE ALL STARS: Autry DeWalt Mixon Jr. (b. 1931 - d. 1995) and band. Rhythm 'n' Blues and Soul singer and saxophonist from Blytheville, Arkansas. 'Shotgun' was a US Pop No. 4 and R&B No. 1, and 'Shake and Fingerpop' a US Pop No. 29 and R&B No. 10. One of Motown's tougher acts, they are excellent on this show.

ROY HEAD: Roy Kent Head (b. 1941 - 2020) Rhythm 'n' blues and country singer from Three Rivers, Texas. 'Treat Her Right' got to No. 2 in the US Pop and the R&B charts. This is the first of 2 'Shindig!' appearances.

GLEN CAMPBELL: 'Universal Soldier' reached No. 45 in the US charts.

CAROLYN JONES: Carolyn Sue Jones (b. 1930 - d. 1983). Actress from Amarillo, Texas, best remembered for her role in 'The Addams Family'. She speaks rather than sings 'This Little Bird'.

L-R: Jackie DeShannon; Junior Walker and The All Stars; Roy Head; The Shindogs; Glen Campbell; Carolyn Jones

Episode 60: 14th October 1965

Opening Medley: **Millie Small** - I'm In Love Again / **Willy Nelson** - Jailer, Bring Me Water / **The Modern Folk Quartet** - One Track Mind / **Donna Loren** - When The Lovelight Starts Shining Through His Eyes / **The Animals** - I'm Crying (End of Medley)
The Modern Folk Quartet - Come On In
Marianne Faithfull - There But For Fortune *
Jim Weatherly - I'm A Happy Man
Millie Small - My Boy Lollipop
The Animals - Boom Boom
Donna Loren - The Way Of Love
The Animals - We Gotta Get Out Of This Place
Billy Preston - Sticks and Stones
Zsa Zsa Gabor with **The Blossoms** and **The Wellingtons** - Hi-Heel Sneakers
The Animals - Bring It On Home To Me
The Animals - Don't Let Me Be Misunderstood
Millie Small - Bloodshot Eyes
Willy Nelson - Sea Cruise
The Animals - Talkin' 'Bout You

MILLIE SMALL: 'I'm In Love Again' is from her album 'Millie Sings Fats Domino', 'My Boy Lollipop' is a 2nd performance of her giant hit, and 'Bloodshot Eyes' got to No. 48 in the UK charts.

ZSA ZSA GABOR: Sári Gábor (b. 1917 - d. 2018). Hungarian-American actress who clearly couldn't sing.

THE ANIMALS: Eric Burdon (Eric Victor Burdon, b. 1941 - vocals), Hilton Valentine (Hilton Stewart Paterson Valentine, b. 1943 - d. 2021 - guitar), Chas Chandler (Bryan James Chandler, b. 1938 - d. 1996 - bass), John Steel (b. 1941 - drums) and Dave Rowberry (David Eric Rowberry, b. 1940 - d. 2003 - keyboards). Rhythm 'n' Blues Group from Newcastle-upon-Tyne, UK. 'I'm Crying' was a US No. 19 and UK No. 8, 'Boom Boom' a US No. 43, 'Don't Let Me Be Misunderstood' a US No. 15 and UK No. 3, 'Bring It On Home To Me' a US No. 32 and UK No. 7, and 'We Gotta Get Out Of This Place' a US No. 13 and UK No. 2. One of the UK's finest bands, they are on great form here, despite the absence of original keyboardist Alan Price. This is the first of 2 'Shindig!' appearances.

THE MODERN FOLK QUARTET: Cyrus Faryar (b. 1936), Henry Diltz (b. 1938), Chip Douglas (Douglas Farthing Hatlelid, b. 1942), and Jerry Yester (Jerome Alan Yester (b. 1943). Folk-Rock group from Greenwich Village, New York City. Jerry Yester would later join The Lovin' Spoonful.

MARIANNE FAITHFULL: Taped in London at least 8 months earlier, Joan Baez's 'There But For Fortune' is a song not released on record.

JIM WEATHERLY: James Dexter Weatherly (b. 1943 - d. 2021). Country and Pop singer from Pontotoc, Mississippi.

WILLY NELSON: 'Sea Cruise' was a 1959 hit for Frankie Ford.

L-R: The Modern Folk Quartet; Marianne Faithfull; Jim Weatherly; Millie Small; The Animals; Zsa Zsa Gabor

Episode 61: 16th October 1965

Ray Peterson, **Kelly Garrett**, **The Lovin' Spoonful**, **Glen Campbell** and **The Shindogs** - Let The Good Times Roll
Jimmy Witherspoon - Love Me Right
Glen Campbell - Kansas City Star
The Lovin' Spoonful - Do You Believe In Magic
Ray Peterson - Yesterday
Kelly Garrett - Tossing and Turning
The Shindogs - Good Golly Miss Molly
Peter and Gordon - Don't Pity Me + To Know You Is To Love You
Vashti - Some Things Just Stick In Your Mind *
The Lovin' Spoonful - Did You Ever Have To Make Up Your Mind?
Glen Campbell and **Ray Peterson** - Slow Down
The Lovin' Spoonful, **Glen Campbell**, **Kelly Garrett**, **The Wellingtons**, **Jimmy Witherspoon** and **Ray Peterson** - When The Saints Go Marching In

NOTE: The available master has been edited, so running order may not be 100% correct!

JIMMY WITHERSPOON: (b. 1920 - d. 1997). Rhythm 'n' Blues and Jazz singer from Gurdon, Arkansas. 'Love Me Right' was his latest single.

THE LOVIN' SPOONFUL: John Sebastian (John Benson Sebastian, b. 1944 - vocals, guitar, harmonica and autoharp), Zal Yanovsky (Zalman Yanovsky, b. 1944 - d. 2002 - guitar and vocals), Steve Boone (b. 1943 - bass) and Jo Butler (Joseph Campbell Butler, b. 1941 - drums and vocals). Folk-Rock and Pop group from Geenwich Village, New York. 'Do You Believe In Magic' was a US No. 9 and 'Did You Ever Have To Make Up Your Mind?' a US No. 2, though both songs flopped in the UK.

PETER AND GORDON: 'To Know You Is To Love You' was a US No. 24 and UK No. 5, and 'Don't Pity Me' was a US No. 83.

VASHTI: Jennifer Vashti Bunyan (b. 1945). Folk and Pop singer from Newcastle-upon-Tyne, UK. Later recorded as Vashti Bunyan. A Jagger-Richards composition, 'Some Things Just Stick in Your Mind' was her debut single. This is the first of 2 'Shindig!' appearances.

L-R: Jimmy Witherspoon; Glen Campbell; Kelly Garrett; Peter and Gordon; Vashti; The Lovin' Spoonful

Episode 62: 21st October 1965

Opening Medley: **The Shindig Band**, **The Blossoms**, **The Kingsmen**, **Eddie Rambeau** and **Joe Tex** - Treat Her Right / **The Kingsmen** - Too Much Monkey Business (End of Medley)
Eddie Rambeau with The Eligibles - Concrete and Clay
Joe Tex - I Want To (Do Everything For You)
Brenda Holloway - Shake
The Kingsmen - Money (That's What I Want)
The Dave Clark Five - Having A Wild Weekend
Brenda Holloway - You Can Cry On My Shoulder
The Kingsmen - Medley: Jolly Green Giant / Annie Fanny / Little Latin Lupe Lu
Eddie Rambeau - The Train
The Kingsmen - Louie Louie
Joe Tex - I've Got A Woman
The Kingsmen, **Joe Tex**, **Brenda Holloway** and **Eddie Rambeau** - Do You Love Me

EDDIE RAMBEAU: 'Concrete and Clay' is another performance of his US No. 35 hit, and 'The Train' was a non-charting single.

JOE TEX: 'I Want To (Do Everything For You)' was a US Pop No. 23 and R&B No. 1. 'I've Got A Woman' is the Ray Charles classic.

THE KINGSMEN: Performed here as part of a medley along with other hits, 'Annie Fanny' was a US No. 47.

THE DAVE CLARK FIVE: 'Having A Wild Weekend' was the US title track of their movie. This performance was taped on the same day as their appearance in Episode 53.

BRENDA HOLLOWAY: Her latest single, 'You Can Cry On My Shoulder' failed to chart.

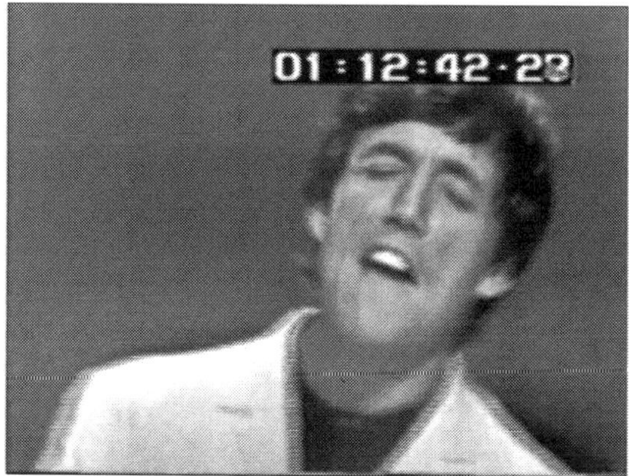

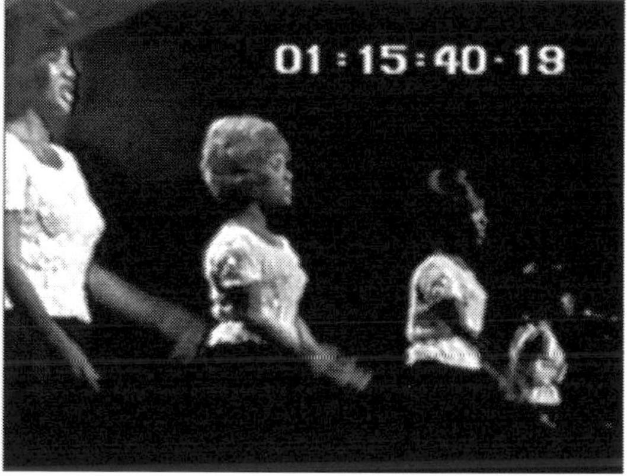

L-R: Eddie Rambeau; Joe Tex; Brenda Holloway; The Kingsmen; The Dave Clark Five; The Blossoms

Episode 63: 23rd October 1965

Opening Medley: **Dobie Gray** - See You At The Go-Go / **The Shangri-Las** - Thirty Days / **The Byrds** - I'm A Loser / **Bobby Sherman** and **Glen Campbell** - Ready Teddy (End of Medley)
The Byrds - Chimes Of Freedom
Dobie Gray - The 'In' Crowd
The Shangri-Las - Right Now and Not Later
The Shindogs - Keep A Knockin'
Glen Campbell - Everyone's Gone To The Moon
The Byrds - Turn! Turn! Turn!
Bobby Sherman - Goody Galum-Shus
The Shangri-Las - Give Him A Great Big Kiss
Dobie Gray - My Baby
Glen Campbell, The Eligibles, Bobby Sherman, The Blossoms, Joey Cooper and Delaney Bramlett - Peppermint Twist
The Shangri-Las, Dobie Gray, Glen Campbell and **Bobby Sherman** - Twist and Shout

THE BYRDS: 'Turn! Turn! Turn!' was a US chart-topper and UK No. 26 hit, and the wonderful 'Chimes Of Freedom' is a song from their 'Mr. Tambourine Man' album.

DOBIE GRAY: 'See You At The Go-Go' was a US No. 9, and 'The 'In' Crowd' is another performance of his big hit.

THE SHANGRI-LAS: Now back to a quartet (Betty Weiss was absent from their earlier 'Shindig!' performance due to temporarily leaving to have a baby) , the Motown-styled 'Right Now and Not Later' peaked at No. 99, while 'Give Him A Great Big Kiss' is another performance of the group's No. 18 hit.

GLEN CAMPBELL: 'Everyone's Gone To The Moon' was a current hit for Jonathan King.

BOBBY SHERMAN: 'Goody Galum-Shus' was released as a non-charting single.

L-R: The Byrds; Dobie Gray; The Shangri-Las; The Shindogs; Glen Campbell; Bobby Sherman

Episode 64: 28th October 1965

Opening Medley: **The Newbeats** - Everything's All Right / **Dinah Lee** - What Kind Of Love Is This / **The Toys** and **Jerry Naylor** - Why Do Fools Fall In Love? / **The Shindogs** - Reelin' and Rockin' (End of Medley)
Dinah Lee - I'm Walkin'
Glen Campbell - Working For The Man
The Toys - A Lover's Concerto
The Newbeats, **The Blossoms** and **The Wellingtons** - Run, Baby Run (Back Into My Arms)
Manfred Mann - One In The Middle *
Jerry Naylor - Everybody Loves A Clown
The Shindogs - Someday Someday
Jack E. Leonard (Guest Host) - I'm Sitting On Top Of The World
Glen Campbell, **Dinah Lee** and **Jerry Naylor** - Road Runner
The Newbeats - Bread and Butter
The Shindogs and **Glen Campbell** - Do You Wanna Dance?

DINAH LEE: Released as a single, Fats Domino's 'I'm Walkin'' was a hit in Australia for this New Zealand-born singer.

GLEN CAMPBELL: 'Working For The Man' was a 1962 hit for Roy Orbison.

THE TOYS: Barbara Harris (Barbara Ann Harris, b. 1945), Barbara Parritt (b. 1944) and June Montiero (b. 1946). Rhythm 'n' Blues and Pop Girl Group from Jamaica, New York. 'A Lover's Concerto' reached No. 2 on the US charts and No. 5 in the UK.

THE NEWBEATS: Their latest single, 'Run, Baby Run (Back Into My Arms)' reached No. 12 in the US and No. 10 in the UK, and 'Bread and Butter' was another performance of their earlier hit.

MANFRED MANN: 'The One In The Middle' was the title track of a No. 1 UK EP, while in the US it was the B-side of the 'If You Gotta Go, Go Now' single.

JACK E. LEONARD: Leonard Lebitsky (b. 1910 - d. 1973). Comedian and Actor from Chicago, Illinois.

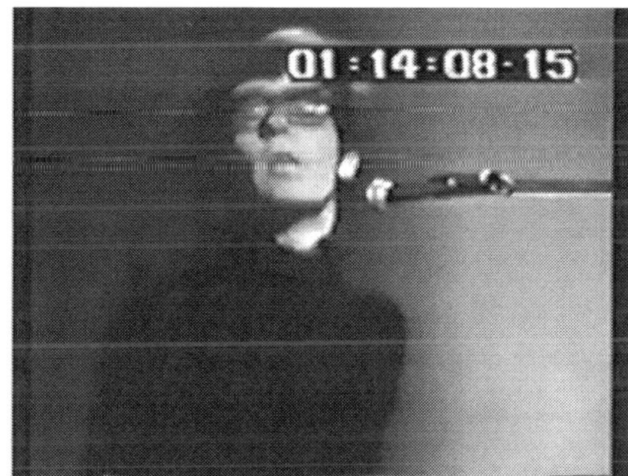

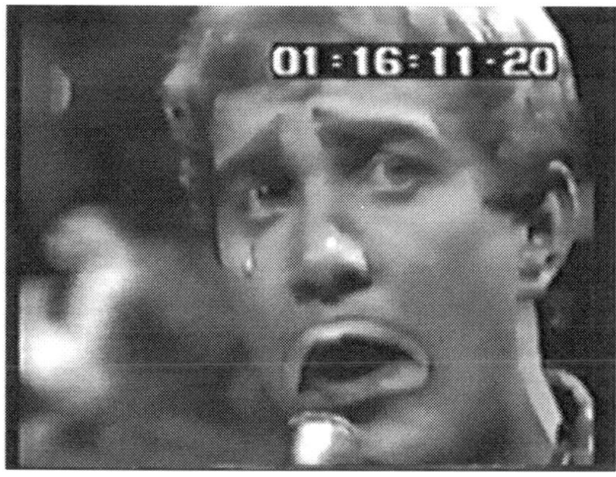

L-R: Dinah Lee; The Toys; The Newbeats; Manfred Mann; Jerry Naylor; Jack E. Leonard

Episode 65: 30th October 1965

Opening Medley: **Billy Preston** - Instrumental / **Bobby Sherman** - Help! / **Bobby Sherman** with **The Wellingtons** - I'm Down / **Jackie and Gayle**, **Ted Cassidy**, **The Blossoms** and **The Spokesmen** - Get On The Right Track Bobby (End of Medley)
Jim Doval and The Gauchos - Tell Me What You're Gonna Do
Jackie and Gayle - Everyone's Gone To The Moon
Bobby Sherman - Memphis
The Spokesmen - There But For Fortune
Boris Karloff - Peppermint Twist
The Wellingtons - Some Enchanted Evening
The Gauchos with **Billy Preston** - Bony Moronie
Bobby Sherman - You Can't Sit Down (Finale, Closing Credits)

Also performed (but missing from the surviving master) were:

Boris Karloff - Monster Mash
Ted Cassidy - The Lurch
Jim Doval and The Gauchos - Out Of Sight + Bella's Bash
Billy Preston with **The Gauchos** - Bony Moronie
The Wellingtons - Scully Gully

BORIS KARLOFF: William Henry Pratt (b. 1887 - d. 1969). Actor from Camberwell, Surrey, UK.

TED CASSIDY: Theodore Crawford Cassidy (b. 1932 - d. 1979). Actor from Pittsburgh, Pennsylvania. Best known for playing Lurch in 'The Adams Family'.

THE SPOKESMEN: John Madara (John Medora, b. 1936), David White (David White Tricker, b. 1939 - d. 2019) and Ray Gilmore. Pop vocal trio from Philadelphia, Pennsylvania. John Madara and David White were previously in Rock 'n' Roll group Danny and The Juniors. 'There But For Fortune' was on their sole album 'The Dawn Of Correction'.

While this Halloween Special is quite good fun, it was also the beginning of a down-turn in quality and a focus on family-friendly entertainment. There would be far more horrifying shows than this!

L-R: Ted Cassidy; Jim Doval and The Gauchos; Jackie and Gayle; The Spokesmen; Boris Karloff; Billy Preston

Episode 66: 4th November 1965

Louis Armstrong Part 1

Louis Armstrong - Sleepy Time Down South
Louis Armstrong - Instrumental
Louis Armstrong - Indiana (Instrumental)
Louis Armstrong - The Bucket's Got A Hole In It
Jewel Brown - I Left My Heart In San Francisco
Louis Armstrong - Instrumental
Louis Armstrong - Blueberry Hill
Louis Armstrong - Hello Dolly
Louis Armstrong - When The Saints Go Marching In

LOUIS ARMSTRONG: Louis Daniel Armstrong (b. 1901 - d. 1971). Jazz and Pop Trumpeter and Vocalist from New Orleans, Louisiana. In 1965 Louis Armstrong was at the peak of his latter-day popularity, thanks in no small part to his 1964 chart-topper 'Hello, Dolly!' (a record which ended The Beatles' 14 week unbroken run at No. 1).

JEWEL BROWN: (b. 1937). Jazz and Blues singer from Houston, Texas. She was a regular part of Louis Armstrong's touring band in the '60s.

While there is no doubting Louis Armstrong's much deserved legendary status, this show didn't appeal at all to the show's usual audience. There was another Episode dedicated to Louis Armstrong a week later.

L-R: Louis Armstrong; Jewel Brown; Louis Armstrong

Episode 67: 6th November 1965

Opening Medley: **Billy Joe Royal** - Down In The Boondocks / **Fontella Bass** - Jim Dandy / **The Strangeloves** - Roll On Mississippi / **Jackie Wilson** - The Way I Am (End of Medley)
The Rolling Stones - Good Times *
Fontella Bass - Rescue Me
The Strangeloves - Cara-Lin
Jackie Wilson - I Believe I'll Love On
Billy Joe Royal - I've Got To Be Somebody
Tony and The Bandits - It's A Bit Of Alright
The Rolling Stones - Have Mercy *
Billy Joe Royal - I Knew You When
Fontella Bass - Everyday I Have To Cry
The Strangeloves - I Want Candy
Jackie Wilson - Baby Workout

BILLY JOE ROYAL: 'Down In The Boondocks' and 'I Knew You When' are both 2nd 'Shindig!' performances of his biggest hits, and 'I've Got To Be Somebody' was a US No. 38.

JACKIE WILSON: 1961's 'The Way I Am' was a US Pop No. 58, his latest single 'I Believe I'll Love On' a US Pop No. 96 and R&B No. 34, and 'Baby Workout' is another performance of his 1963 US Pop No. 5 and R&B chart-topper.

THE ROLLING STONES: Seen here in a performance taped in London on 28th July 1965, Sam Cooke's 'Good Times' was released on both the US and UK versions of 'Out Of Our Heads' album, as was their cover of Don Covay's 'Mercy, Mercy'.

FONTELLA BASS: Fontella Marie Bass (b. 1940, d. 2012). Rhythm 'n' Blues and Soul singer from St. Louis, Missouri. 'Rescue Me' got to No. 4 in the US Pop charts, No. 1 in R&B and No. 11 in the UK.

THE STRANGELOVES: Bob Feldman, Jerry Goldstein and Richard Gottehrer. Pop and Rock trio from New York City. 'I Want Candy' was a US No. 7, and 'Cara-Lin' got to No. 39.

TONY AND THE BANDITS: Tony Brazis (Anthony Joseph Brazis - vocals and guitar), Bill Bartlett (William Bartlett, b. 1946 - guitar), Bob Dudak (bass) and Bill Albaugh (William E. Albaugh, b. 1946 - d. 1999 - drums). Garage band from Cincinatti, Ohio. Appearing on the show because they had won a competition, this didn't prevent their single of 'It's A Bit Of Alright' from failing to chart.

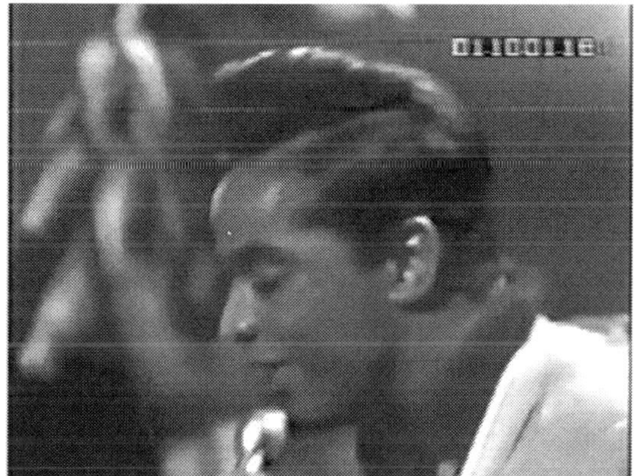

L-R: The Rolling Stones; Fontella Bass; The Strangeloves; Jackie Wilson; Billy Joe Royal; Tony and The Bandits

Episode 68: 11th November 1965

Louis Armstrong Part 2

Louis Armstrong - Sleepy Time Down South
Louis Armstrong - Struttin' With Some Barbeque
Louis Armstrong - I've Got A Lot Of Living To Do
Tyree Glenn - Avalon
Jewel Brown - My Man
Louis Armstrong - Mack The Knife
Louis Armstrong - Ole Miss
Louis Armstrong - I've Got A Lot Of Living To Do (Reprise)

TYREE GLENN: William Tyree Glenn (b. 1912 - d. 1974). Jazz trombone and vibraphone player from New Jersey.

Another show that was aimed at moms and dads. A shame really, as in the right context this is a great performance.

L-R: Louis Armstrong; Jewel Brown; Louis Armstrong

Episode 69: 13th November 1965

The Righteous Brothers - Justine
Donna Loren - Where Have All The Flowers Gone?
Rick Nelson - Live and Learn
Barbara Lewis - Make Me Your Baby
The Turtles - Your Maw Said You Cried (In Your Sleep Last Night)
The Righteous Brothers - Guess Who?
David Jones - What Are We Going To Do?
The Turtles - Let Me Be
Roy Head - Treat Her Right
Rick Nelson - I Catch Myself Crying
Barbara Lewis - Baby I'm Yours
The Righteous Brothers - Fannie Mae
Roy Head - Apple Of My Eye
The Gentrys - Keep On Dancing

RICK NELSON: Eric Hilliard Nelson (b. 1940, d. 1985). Rock 'n' roll and pop singer from Teaneck, New Jersey. Billed as 'Ricky Nelson' up until May 1961. 'Live and Learn' is from his 1964 album 'Spotlight On Rick', and 'I Catch Myself Crying' is from 1965's 'Love and Kisses'.

BARBARA LEWIS: 'Make Me Your Baby' and 'Baby I'm Yours' were both US No. 11 Pop hits.

THE TURTLES: 'Let Me Be' was a US No. 29 hit, and 'Your Maw Said You Cried (In Your Sleep Last Night)' was its B-side.

DAVID JONES: David Thomas Jones (b. 1945 - d. 2012). Pop singer from Manchester, UK. 'What Are We Going To Do?' was a minor US hit at No. 93. He would find far greater success (as 'Davy Jones') in The Monkees.

ROY HEAD: 'Treat Her Right' is another performance of his big hit, and 'Apple Of My Eye' peaked at No. 32 in the US charts.

THE GENTRYS: Larry Raspberry (vocals and guitar), Bruce Bowles (vocals), Jimmy Hart (vocals), Bobby Fisher (saxophone and keyboards), Jimmy Johnson (trumpet), Pat Neal (bass guitar) and Larry Wall (drums). Pop group from Memphis, Tennessee. 'Keep On Dancing' was a US No. 4 hit.

L-R: Barbara Lewis; The Turtles; The Righteous Brothers; David Jones; Rick Nelson; The Gentrys

Episode 70: 18th November 1965

'The Wild Weird World of Dr. Goldfoot'

Harvey Lembeck - It Works
Aron Kincaid and **Susan Hart** - What's A Boy Supposed To Do?

VINCENT PRICE: Vincent Leonard Price Jr. (b. 1911 - d. 1993). Actor from St. Louis, Missouri.

TOMMY KIRK: Thomas Lee Kirk (b. 1941). Actor from Louisville, Kentucky.

SUSAN HART: Susan Neidhart (b. 1941). Actress from Wenatchee, Washington.

ARON KINCAID: Norman Neale Williams II (b. 1940 - d. 2011). Actor from Los Angeles, California.

HARVEY LEMBECK: (b. 1923 - d. 1982). Actor from Brooklyn, New York City.

A daft James Bond spoof starring Vincent Price, Tommy Kirk, Susan Hart, Aron Kincaid and Harvey Lembeck, this has nothing whatsoever to do with 'Shindig!' apart from the name. There were also two Dr. Goldfoot movies, 'Dr. Goldfoot and The Bikini Machine' in 1965 and the following year's 'Dr. Goldfoot and The Girl Bombs'.

L-R: Aron Kincaid; Tommy Kirk and Susan Hart; Vincent Price

Episode 71: 20th November 1965

Shindig In Hawaii Part 1

Don Ho and The Aliis - I'll Remember You
Len Barry - 1-2-3
Donna Loren - Take Me In Your Arms (Rock Me A Little While)
Ian Whitcomb - You Turn Me On (Turn On Song)
Tommy Sands - The Statue
Billy Preston - Ain't That Peculiar?
The Shindogs - I Live For The Sun
Bobby Sherman and **Donna Loren** - Roses and Rainbows
Donna Loren - My Heart Sings
Tommy Sands - Just A Little Bit Better
Ian Whitcomb - That's Rock 'N' Roll
Bobby Sherman - Honolulu Lulu

DON HO AND THE ALIIS: Donald Tai Loy Ho (b. 1930 - d. 2007), Al Akana, Rudy Aquino, Benny Chong, Manny Lagodlagod and Joe Mundo. Pop singer and pianist with backing band from Honolulu, Hawaii. This is the first of 2 'Shindig!' appearances.

LEN BARRY: Leonard Borisoff (b. 1942 - d. 2020). Soul and pop singer from Philadelphia, Pennsylvania. A former member of The Dovells, '1-2-3' peaked at No. 2 in the US charts and No. 3 in the UK. The first of 2 'Shindig!' appearances.

IAN WHITCOMB: As well as his biggest hit 'You Turn Me On (Turn On Song)', performed here is an unimpressive version of The Coasters' 'That's Rock 'N' Roll'.

TOMMY SANDS: Thomas Adrian Sands (b. 1937). Pop and Country singer from Chicago, Illinois. 'The Statue' was his latest single, and 'Just A Little Bit Better' was Herman's Hermits' current hit.

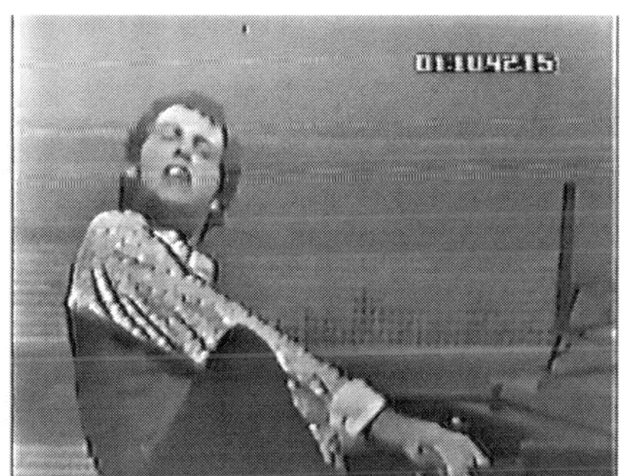

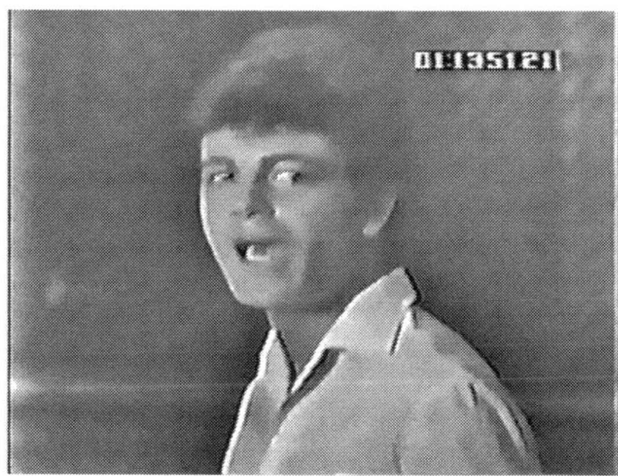

L-R: Don Ho and Aliis; Len Barry; Donna Loren; Ian Whitcomb; Tommy Sands; The Shindogs

Episode 72: 25th November 1965

Shindig In Hawaii Part 2

Opening Medley: **Glen Campbell** - Hidden Island / **The Wellingtons** - Ride The Wild Surf / **James Burton** - Yakety Sax / **Glen Campbell** - 12th Street Rag (End of Medley)
Bobby Sherman - The Pied Piper
The Wellingtons - Chapel In The Moonlight
Dodie Marshall with **The Blossoms** - Round Every Corner
Len Barry and **Glen Campbell** with **The Blossoms** - Ring Dang Doo
Don Ho and Aliis - Pearly Shells
The Blossoms - I Hear A Symphony
Glen Campbell with **The Wellingtons** - May The Bird Of Paradise Fly Up Your Nose
Ian Whitcomb - Rolling Home To Georgette
Dodie Marshall - Where Do You Go?
Len Barry - Lip Synch
The Shindogs - Kansas City
Don Ho - Aloha Oe

BOBBY SHERMAN: 'The Pied Piper' was a current hit for the UK's Crispian St. Peters, though Bobby Sherman actually sounds more like Sonny Bono.

DODIE MARSHALL: (b. 1934). Actress and singer from London, UK and raised in Philadelphia. Best known for appearing in the Elvis Presley movies 'Spinout' in 1966 and 'Easy Come, Easy Go' in 1967. 'Where Do You Go?' was a hit for Cher.

LEN BARRY: 'Lip Sync' was a No. 84 US hit, and 'Ring Dang Doo' was a single for Sam The Sham and The Pharaohs.

THE BLOSSOMS: With lead vocals by Darlene Love, 'I Hear A Symphony' is a fine cover of The Supremes' hit.

L-R: James Burton; Glen Campbell; Bobby Sherman; The Wellingtons; Dodie Marshall; Len Barry and Glen Campbell

Episode 73: 27th November 1965

George Maharis - Medley: King Of The Road / Route 66
George Maharis - Medley: Witchcraft / My Kind Of Girl / I Can't Believe That You're In Love With Me
The Young Americans - Medley: Yankee Doodle / Dixie / This Land Is Your Land
George Maharis - It's Not Unusual
The Young Americans - Medley of songs by individual members
George Maharis - Oh Lonesome Me
George Maharis - Here's That Rainy Day
The Young Americans - Medley: Waiting For The Robert E. Lee / Swanee
George Maharis and **The Young Americans** - Carolina In The Morning
The Young Americans - Hambone
George Maharis and **The Young Americans** - Swanee
George Maharis - Medley: God Bless The Child / He's Got The Whole World In His Hands

GEORGE MAHARIS: (b. 1928). Actor and singer from Queens, New York, best known for his role in 'Route 66'.

THE YOUNG AMERICANS: Pop and Broadway choir and musicians from California.

After two mediocre shows filmed in Hawaii, comes something far, far worse. 'Shindig!'s nadir.

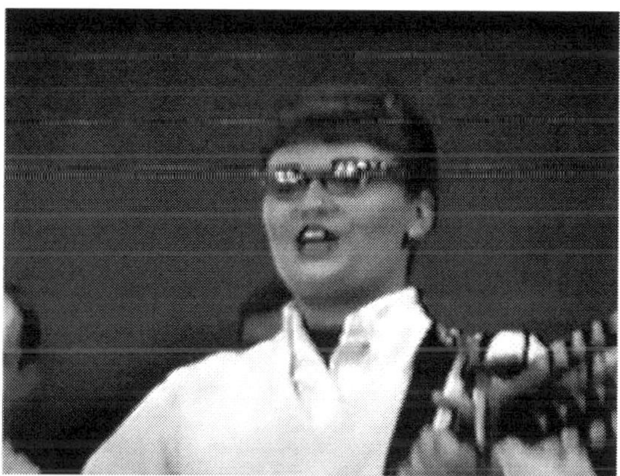

L-R: Jimmy O'Neill (Presenter); The Young Americans; George Maharis

Episode 74: 2nd December 1965

Opening Medley: **Leroy Van Dyke** - The Auctioneer / **Gloria Jones** - Puppy Love / **Bobby Sherman** - Wake Up Little Susie / **We Five** - Green Green

Leroy Van Dyke - It's All Over Now, Baby Blue

Gloria Jones - Heartbeat

We Five - You Were On My Mind

Bobby Sherman - New Orleans

The Hollies - Look Through Any Window *

Tommy Turner - Aware Of Love

Melody Patterson - You're The One

We Five - Get Together

The Searchers - Needles and Pins *

Leroy Van Dyke - Walk On By

Bobby Sherman and **Billy Preston** - Lucille

We Five, **Bobby Sherman**, **Melody Patterson** and **The Blossoms** - He's Got The Whole World In His Hands

LEROY VAN DYKE: Performed on the show for the 2nd time, 'The Auctioneer' reached US Pop No. 19 and C&W No. 9, and 'Walk On By' No. 5 Pop and No. 1 C&W. Bob Dylan's 'It's All Over Now, Baby Blue' sounds not unlike Johnny Cash.

GLORIA JONES: Gloria Richetta Jones (b. 1945). Soul singer and pianist from Cincinnati, Ohio. 'Heartbeat' got to No. 128 in the US charts.

WE FIVE: 'You Were On My Mind' is a 2nd performance of their US No. 3 hit. Crispian St. Peters had major success with the song in the UK.

THE HOLLIES: 'Look Through Any Window' got to No. 32 in the US and No. 4 in the UK. This performance was taped on the same day as their appearance in Episode 56.

TOMMY TURNER: Rhythm 'n' Blues and Soul singer, who was formerly in a couple of groups with Jewel Akens.

MELODY PATTERSON: (b. 1949 - d. 2015). Actress and singer from Inglewood, California. Best known for her role in 'F Troop', 'You're The One' was her only single.

THE SEARCHERS: Already an oldie by late 1965, 'Needles and Pins' was a US No. 13 and UK No. 1 hit in early 1964.

L-R: Gloria Jones; We Five; The Hollies; Tommy Turner; Melody Patterson; The Searchers

Episode 75: 4th December 1965

Shindig Goes To London Part 1

(Filmed at The Richmond on-Thames Jazz Festival)

The Animals - Rosie *
The Animals - We Gotta Get Outta This Place *
The Moody Blues - I'll Go Crazy *
The Brian Auger Trinity - Do Lord Remember Me *
Gary Farr and The T-Bones - Wooly Bully *
Georgie Fame and The Blue Flames - Monkeying Around *
The Brian Auger Trinity with **Eric Burdon** and **Stevie Winwood** - I Feel Alright *

THE ANIMALS: An old prison work song, 'Rosie' was later rewritten as 'Inside-Looking Out', a US No. 34 and UK No. 12 hit for the group, while 'We Gotta Get Outta This Place' is another version of their US No. 13 and UK No. 2. The Animals' performance was taped on 8th August 1965.

THE MOODY BLUES: Taped on 6th August 1965, 'I'll Go Crazy' is a different performance to the one in Episode 35.

THE BRIAN AUGER TRINITY (THE STEAMPACKET): Long John Baldry (John William Baldry, b. 1941 - d. 2005 - vocals), Rod Stewart (Roderick David Stewart, b. 1945 - vocals), Julie Driscoll (b. 1947 - vocals), Brian Auger (Brian Albert Gordon Auger, b. 1939 - organ), Vic Briggs (Victor Harvey Briggs III, b. 1945 - guitar), Ricky Fenson (Richard Brown, b. 1945 - bass) and Micky Waller (Michael Waller, b. 1941 - d. 2008 - drums). Rhythm 'n' Blues and Soul band from London. Billed on-screen as 'The Brian Auger Trinity', the group featured is in fact The Steampacket, though to confuse matters even more the show's original posters named the band as "The Steam Packet with The Brian Auger Trinity, Rod Stewart, Julie Driscoll and Long John Baldry". Due to contractual reasons The Steampacket never properly recorded or released any music during their short life-span. This performance was taped on 8th August 1965. For the show's finale, the group are joined by Eric Burdon and Stevie Winwood, lead singers for The Animals and The Spencer Davis Group, respectively.

GARY FARR AND THE T-BONES: Gary Farr (b. 1944 - d. 1994 - vocals), Winston Weatherill (guitar), Andy McKechnie (guitar) Stuart Parkes (bass) and Brian Walkley (drums). Rhythm 'n' Blues group from Worthing, Sussex, UK. Their cover of the Sam the Sham and the Pharaohs' 'Wooly Bully' wasn't released on record. The performance was taped on 7th August 1965.

GEORGIE FAME AND THE BLUE FLAMES: In a performance taped on 7th August 1965, 'Monkeying Around' is a song from the UK 'Fame At Last' and US 'Yeh Yeh' albums.

This and part 2 (broadcast 5 days later) are amongst the most exciting shows ever broadcast under the 'Shindig!' name, and it's a real shame there weren't more like it.

L-R: The Animals; The Moody Blues; The Brian Auger Trinity; Gary Farr and The T-Bones; Georgie Fame and The Blue Flames; The Brian Auger Trinity

Episode 76: 9th December 1965

Shindig Goes To London Part 2

(Filmed at The Richmond-on-Thames Jazz Festival)

The Yardbirds - For Your Love *
The Yardbirds - Hang On Sloopy *
Manfred Mann - If You Gotta Go, Go Now *
The Graham Bond Organisation - Hoochie Koochie Man *
The Who - Anyway, Anyhow, Anywhere *
The Who - Shout and Shimmy *

THE YARDBIRDS: Taped on 6th August, 'For Your Love' is another performance of their US No. 6 and UK No. 3 hit, and 'My Girl Sloopy' is on the US 'For Your Love' album. Curiously, colour footage of this performance recently surfaced, despite all 'Shindig!' broadcasts being in black and white. Could the entire 'Shindig Goes to London' shows survive in colour?

MANFRED MANN: 'If You Gotta Go, Go Now' flopped in the US but got to No. 2 in the UK. Seen here in a performance taped on 7th August 1965, the line "Or else you got to stay all night" is censored.

THE GRAHAM BOND ORGANISATION: Graham Bond (Graham John Clifton Bond, b. 1937 - d. 1974 - vocals and keyboards), Jack Bruce (John Symon Asher Bruce, b. 1943 - d. 2014 - bass), Ginger Baker (Peter Edward Baker, b. 1939 - d. 2019 - drums) and Dick Heckstall-Smith (Richard Malden Heckstall-Smith, b. 1934 - d. 2004 - saxophone). Rhythm 'n' Blues group from London. Seen here in a performance taped on 7th August 1965, 'Hoochie Koochie Man' is a track from their 'The Sound of '65' album.

THE WHO: 'Anyway, Anyhow, Anywhere' was a UK No. 10 hit, and 'Shout and Shimmy' was the UK B-side of 'My Generation'. This astonishing performance was taped on 6th August 1965.

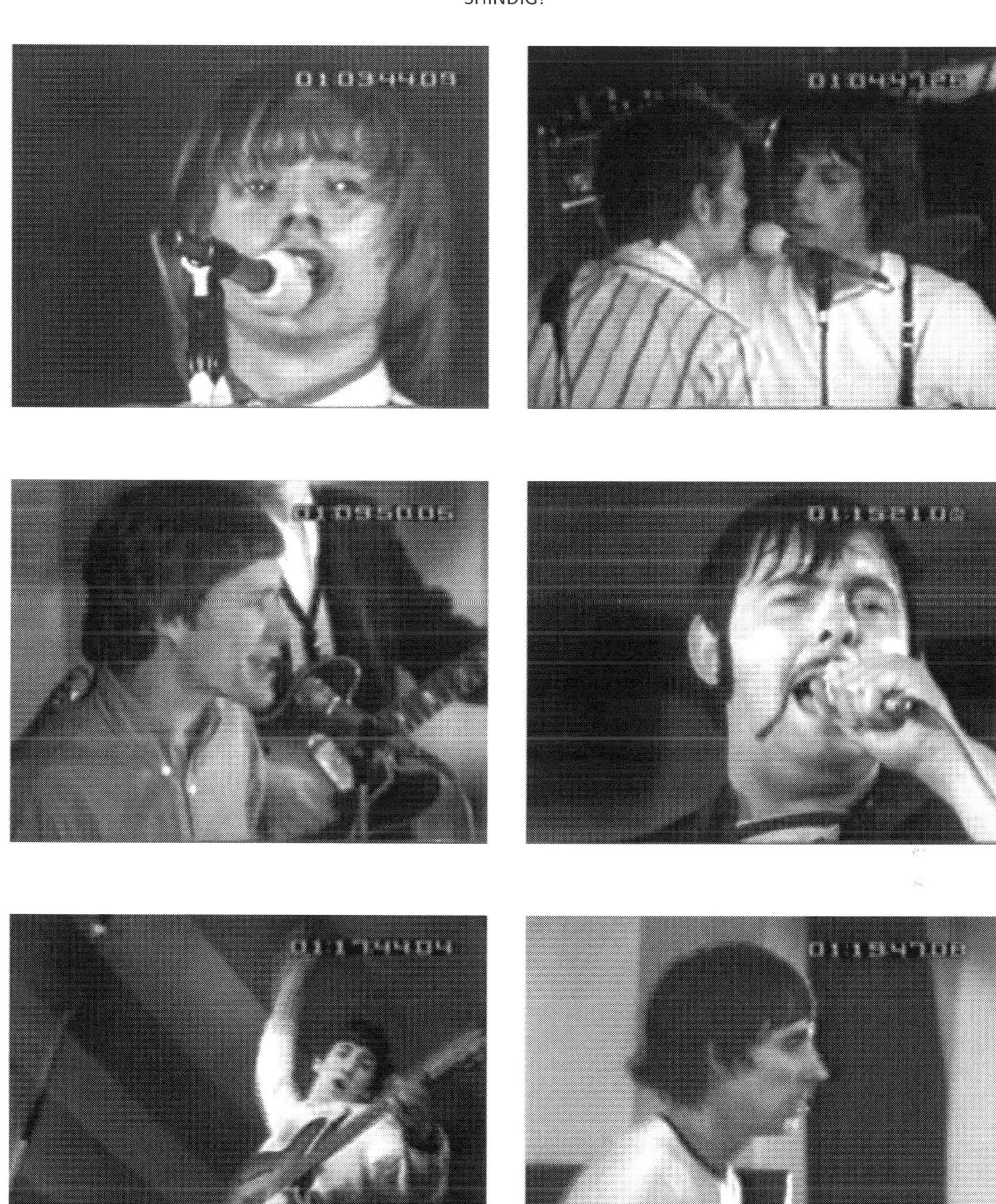

L-R: The Yardbirds (x2); Manfred Mann; The Graham Bond Organisation; The Who (x2)

Episode 77: 11th December 1965

Barry McGuire and **The Grassroots** - Out Of Sight
Barry McGuire - She Belongs To Me
The Grass Roots - Ain't That Lovin You Baby
Barry McGuire with **The Mamas and The Papas** - Yesterday
The Mamas and The Papas - I Call Your Name
The Mamas and The Papas with **The Grass Roots** - Somebody Groovy
Barry McGuire with **The Mamas and The Papas** - Do You Believe In Magic?
Barry McGuire with **The Mamas and The Papas** - You've Got To Hide Your Love Away
The Mamas and The Papas - California Dreamin'
Barry McGuire - This Precious Time
Barry McGuire with **The Mamas and The Papas** - Hang On Sloopy

BARRY McGUIRE: (b. 1935). Folk-Rock singer and guitarist from California. 'This Precious Time' was his latest single. James Brown's 'Out Of Sight' is totally unsuited to him, unlike Bob Dylan's 'She Belongs To Me' which sounds tailor-made.

THE GRASS ROOTS: Willie Fulton (Willie James Fulton - guitar and vocals), Denny Ellis (guitar and vocals), David Stensen (bass and vocals) and Joel Larson (b. 1947 - drums). Folk-Rock band from Los Angeles, California.

THE MAMAS AND THE PAPAS: Cass Elliot (Ellen Naomi Cohen, b. 1941 - d. 1974), John Phillips (John Edmund Andrew Phillips, b. 1935 - d. 2001), Denny Doherty (Dennis Gerrard Stephen Doherty, b. 1940 - d. 2007) and Michelle Phillips (Holly Michelle Gilliam, b. 1944). Folk-Rock and Pop group from Los Angeles, California. 'California Dreamin'' reached No. 4 in the US and No. 9 in the UK, while 'Somebody Groovy' and their cover of The Beatles' 'I Call Your Name' would both appear on their debut album 'If You Can Believe Your Eyes and Ears'.

L-R: Barry McGuire (x2); The Grass Roots (x2); The Mamas and The Papas (x2)

Episode 78: 16th December 1965

The Yardbirds - Heart Full Of Soul *
Jackie Lee (with **The Blossoms**) - The Duck
Vashti Bunyan - I Want To Be Alone *
The Pretty Things - Big City *
Elkie Brooks - Strange Tho' It Seems *
Unit 4 + 2 - Concrete and Clay *
Lulu and The Luvvers - I'll Come Running Over *
Georgie Fame and The Blue Flames - Monkeying Around *
Gloria Jones - Heartbeat
The Yardbirds - I'm A Man *

THE YARDBIRDS: 'Heart Full Of Soul' is a repeat of the performance in Episode 54, while Bo Diddley's 'I'm A Man' appeared on the UK 'Five Live Yardbirds' and on the US 'Having A Rave Up with The Yardbirds' albums (actually *twice* on the latter album).

JACKIE LEE: Earl Lee Nelson (b. 1928 - d. 2008). Rhythm 'n' Blues and Soul singer from Lake Charles who also performed as 'Earl Nelson' in the duo Bob and Earl. 'The Duck' was a US No. 14 Pop hit and No. 4 in R&B.

VASHTI: 'I Want To Be Alone' was the B-side of Vashti's debut single 'Some Things Just Stick in Your Mind'.

THE PRETTY THINGS: A song from their debut album, it was taped on the same day as the performance in Episode 54.

ELKIE BROOKS: Taped the same day as her previous 'Shindig!' appearance 14 months earlier, 'Strange Tho' It Seems' is the B-side of 'Nothing Left To Do But Cry'.

UNIT 4 + 2: Brian Parker (Brian William Parker, b. 1940 - d. 2001 - vocals and guitar), Tommy Moeller (Thomas John George Moeller, b. 1945 - vocals, guitar and piano), Russ Ballard (Russell Glyn Ballard, b. 1945 - guitar and vocals), Buster Meikle (David Ian Meikle, b. 1942 - vocals and guitar), Pete Moules (Peter Charles Moules, b. 1944 - bass and vocals) and Bob Henrit (Robert John Henrit, b. 1944 - drums). Pop Group from Hertfordshire. 'Concrete and Clay' got to No. 28 in the US charts and No. 1 in the UK.

LULU: Marie McDonald McLaughlin Lawrie (b. 1948). Rhythm 'n' Blues and Pop singer from Glasgow, Scotland. 'I'll Come Running Over' (sometimes called 'I'll Come Running') got to No. 105 in the US but failed completely in the UK.

GEORGIE FAME AND THE BLUE FLAMES: Another performance of his UK 'Fame At Last' and US 'Yeh Yeh' album track.

GLORIA JONES: A 2nd performance of her minor hit 'Heartbeat', this time with Billy Preston backing her on organ.

Some very fine performances here, even though very little was actually performed in the 'Shindig!' studio.

L-R: Jackie Lee; The Pretty Things; Elkie Brooks; Unit 4 + 2; Lulu and The Luvvers; Georgie Fame and The Blue Flames

Episode 79: 18th December 1965

Shindig In Europe Part 1

George Chakiris (Guest Host) - Witchcraft
Orson Welles - So Many Things To Remember
Dizzy Gillespie - Bavarian Beer Guru
Douglas Fairbanks Jr. and **Pamela Franklin** - A scene from 'Romeo and Juliet'
Rita Pavone - Supercalifragilisticexpialidocious
Can Can Dancers at Moylin Rouge, Paris

GEORGE CHAKIRIS: (b. 1934). Singer and actor from Norwood, Ohio. Best known for his role in 'West Side Story', this is the first of 2 'Shindig!' Episodes where he both hosts and performs in the show.

ORSON WELLES: George Orson Welles (b. 1915 - d. 1985). Actor and Director from Kenosha, Wisconsin.

DIZZY GILLESPIE: John Birks Gillespie (b. 1917 - d. 1993). Jazz trumpeter from Cheraw, South Carolina.

DOUGLAS FAIRBANKS JR.: Douglas Elton Fairbanks Jr. (b. 1909 - d. 2000). Actor from New York City.

RITA PAVONE: She released 'Supercalifragilisticexpialidocious' as a European single under the slightly different title of 'Supercalifragilistic Espiralidoso'.

More of a documentary than a show, this is another Episode that isn't worthy of the 'Shindig!' name. The fact that it is a two-parter just rubs salt into the wound.

L-R: Can Can Dancers; Dizzy Gillespie; Douglas Fairbanks Jr. and Pamela Franklin; Rita Pavone; George Chakiris; Orson Welles

Episode 80: 23rd December 1965

The Dave Clark Five - Medley: Zip-A-Dee-Doo-Dah / Can't You See That She's Mine?
Gerry and The Pacemakers - Jambalaya *
Billy J. Kramer with The Dakotas - Trains and Boats and Planes *
Ian Whitcomb - High Blood Pressure
Ann Sydney - The Boy In The Woolly Sweater *
The Moody Blues - I'll Go Crazy *
The Yardbirds - I Wish You Would *
The Wellingtons - Go Ahead and Cry
Lulu and The Luvvers - Shout *

THE DAVE CLARK FIVE: This is a repeat of the performance in Episode 15.

GERRY AND THE PACEMAKERS: 'Jambalaya' is a track from the US 'Second Album' and UK 'How Do You Like It?' albums.

BILLY J. KRAMER AND THE DAKOTAS: Billy J. Kramer's excellent version of Burt Bacharach's 'Trains and Boats and Planes' was a US No. 47 and UK No. 12.

IAN WHITCOMB: 'High Blood Pressure' was his latest, non-charting, single. The song was originally by Huey 'Piano' Smith.

ANN SYDNEY: Ann Sidney (b. 1944). Actress and 1964 'Miss World' winner from Poole, Dorset, UK. 'The Boy In The Woolly Sweater' was her single during a very brief attempt at a music career.

THE MOODY BLUES: Incredibly for just an album track, 'I'll Go Crazy' is the 3rd 'Shindig!' performance of the song.

THE YARDBIRDS: The A-side of the group's first single, this performance was taped on the same day as those in Episodes 54 and 78.

LULU: Taped on the same day as the performance in show 78, Lulu's debut single 'Shout' peaked at No. 94 in the US and No. 7 in the UK.

Another show largely compiled of footage pre-taped in London.

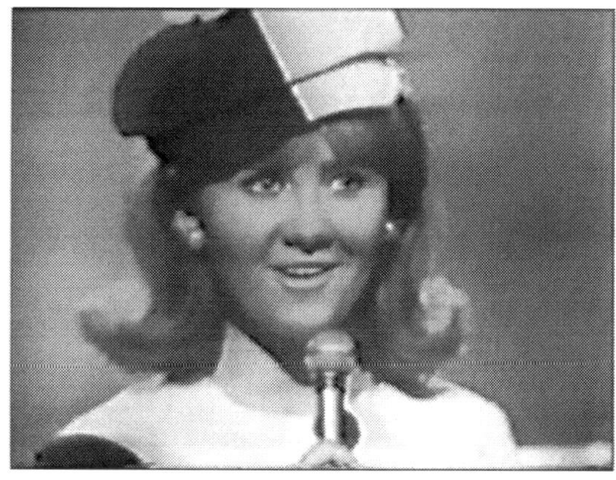

L-R: Gerry and The Pacemakers; Billy J Kramer with The Dakotas; Ann Sydney; The Moody Blues; The Yardbirds; Lulu and The Luvvers

Episode 81: 25th December 1965

Johnny Mathis - On A Wonderful Day Like Today
Johnny Mathis - Misty
Johnny Mathis - Maria
Johnny Mathis - Tonight, Tonight
Johnny Mathis and **Our Young Generation** - Christmas Medley: Marshmallow World / Rudolph, The Red Nose Reindeer / Winter Wonderland / Carol Of The Bells / Ding Dong Merrily On High
Johnny Mathis -Sounds Of Christmas
Johnny Mathis - I'll Be Home For Christmas
Our Young Generation - Hey Look Me Over
Johnny Mathis and **Our Young Generation** - The Sweetheart Tree
Johnny Mathis - Moon River
Johnny Mathis and **Our Young Generation** - Hey Look Me Over
Johnny Mathis - Silent Night

JOHNNY MATHIS: John Royce Mathis (b. 1935). Pop and Easy Listening singer from Gilmer, Texas. 'Misty' got to No. 12 in both the US and UK in 1959, 'Maria' was a US No. 78 in 1960, and 'Winter Wonderland' a UK No. 17 in 1958.

OUR YOUNG GENERATION: Group of teenage singers and musicians, possibly put together especially for this show.

The 1964 Christmas edition of 'Shindig!' featured The Beach Boys, Marvin Gaye, The Righteous Brothers, Donna Loren and Adam Faith; The 1965 show was devoted to Johnny Mathis. Enough said.

L-R: Johnny Mathis (x3)

Episode 82: 30th December 1965

The Hollies - Too Much Monkey Business *
Manfred Mann - Watermelon Man *
The Blossoms - That's When The Tears Start
Georgie Fame and The Blue Flames - Yeh, Yeh
The Who - Daddy Rolling Stone *
Marianne Faithfull - There But For Fortune *
The Hollies - Just One Look *
Adam Faith - Don't You Dig This Kind Of Beat *
Gerry and The Pacemakers - Ferry Cross The Mersey *
Manfred Mann - 5-4-3-2-1 *
The Kinks - Milk Cow Blues *

THE HOLLIES: With lead vocals on 'Too Much Monkey Business' shared between the 3 singers, Graham Nash amusingly throws in an excerpt of The Beatles' 'I Feel Fine'. 'Just One Look' peaked at No. 98 in the US and No. 2 in the UK. This performance was taped on the same day as their appearances in Episodes 56 and 74.

MANFRED MANN: An early theme tune for the UK 'Ready, Steady, Go!' TV show, '5-4-3-2-1' was a No. 5 UK hit.

GEORGIE FAME AND THE BLUE FLAMES: 'Yeh Yeh' was a US No. 21 and UK chart-topper.

THE WHO: The UK B-side of 'Anyway, Anyhow, Anywhere', this performance was taped in London on 3rd August 1965.

MARIANNE FAITHFULL: This is a repeat of the performance in Episode 60.

ADAM FAITH: This is a repeat of the performance in Episode 18.

GERRY AND THE PACEMAKERS: This is a repeat of the performance in Episode 57.

THE KINKS: This performance was taped in London on 4th August 1965.

L-R: The Hollies; Manfred Mann; The Blossoms; Georgie Fame and The Blue Flames; The Who; The Kinks

Episode 83: 1st January 1966

Shindig In Europe Part 2

George Chakiris (Guest Host) and a Woman Dancing
Footage Of Moulin Rouge Dancers
Françoise Hardy - Ce Petit Coeur
George Chakiris - What's New Pussycat? (with **Liana Orfei** at the Colosseum in Rome)
Dancers Shown Rehearsing At Club Pigalle In London
George Chakiris - Name Of The Game Is Love
Shirley Bassey - A Lot Of Living To Do, He Loves Me and It's Yourself *
Closing Comments By George Chakiris and Liana Orfei

FRANÇOISE HARDY: Françoise Madeleine Hardy (b. 1944). Pop singer from Paris, France. 'Ce Petit Coeur' is a track from her 1965 album 'L'amitié.

SHIRLEY BASSEY: Shirley Veronica Bassey (b. 1937). Pop and Jazz singer from Cardiff, Wales, UK. 'It's Yourself' peaked at No. 38 in the US charts.

With the possible exception of Françoise Hardy, this is more showbiz glitz that is the very antithesis of Jack Good's early shows.

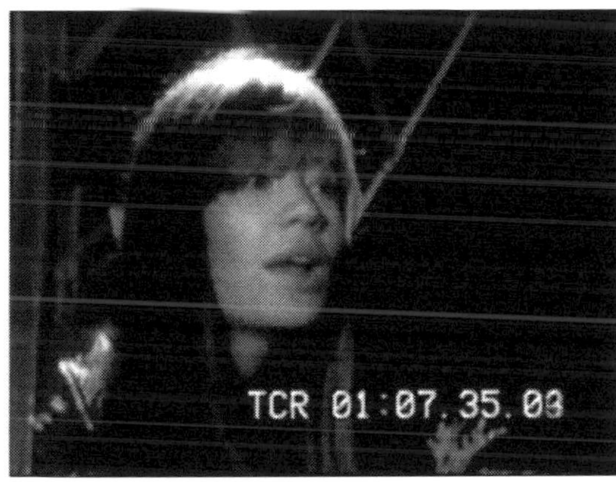

L-R: George Chakiris; Moulin Rouge Dancers; Françoise Hardy; George Chakiris and Liana Orfei; George Chakiris and Dancers; Shirley Bassey

Episode 84: 6th January 1966

Billy J. Kramer with The Dakotas - My Babe *
The Who - I Can't Explain *
Dave Berry - Little Things *
Ian Whitcomb - Robinson Crusoe
Sandie Shaw - Long Live Love *
The Kinks - I Gotta Move *
The Barron Knights - Pop Go The Workers *
Twinkle - Boy Of My Dreams *
The Who - My Generation *
Ian Whitcomb - Hound Dog

BILLY J. KRAMER AND THE DAKOTAS: This was taped on the same day as the performance in Episode 80.

THE WHO: 'I Can't Explain' is a repeat of the performance in Episode 57, and 'My Generation' was a US No. 74 and UK No. 2. This performance of 'My Generation' lacks the usual exciting climax.

DAVE BERRY: Bobby Goldsboro's 'Little Things' was a UK No. 5 hit for Dave Berry.

SANDIE SHAW: A UK chart-topper, 'Long Live Love' stalled at No. 97 in the USA.

THE KINKS: This performance was taped in London on 4th August 1965.

THE BARRON KNIGHTS: Duke D'Mond (Richard Edward Palmer, b. 1943 - d. 2009 - vocals), Butch Baker (Leslie John Baker, b. 1941 - guitar and vocals), Peter Langford (b. 1943 - guitar, keyboards and vocals), Barron Antony (Antony Michael John Osmond, b. 1934 - bass and vocals) and Dave Ballinger (David Alan Ballinger, b. 1939 - drums). Beat and Pop group from Leighton Buzzard, Bedfordshire, UK. Featuring spoofs of The Rolling Stones, Freddie and The Dreamers and The Supremes, 'Pop Go The Workers' got to No. 5 in the UK charts.

TWINKLE: Lynn Annette Ripley (b. 1948 - d. 2015). Pop singer from Surbiton, Surrey, UK. 'The Boy Of My Dreams' was the B-side of her No. 5 UK hit 'Terry', a song that was banned by the BBC and perhaps also considered unsuitable for US TV viewing.

This show looks and sounds more like 'Ready, Steady, Go!' than 'Shindig!'. Not such a bad thing compared to some of the low-lights of recent weeks.

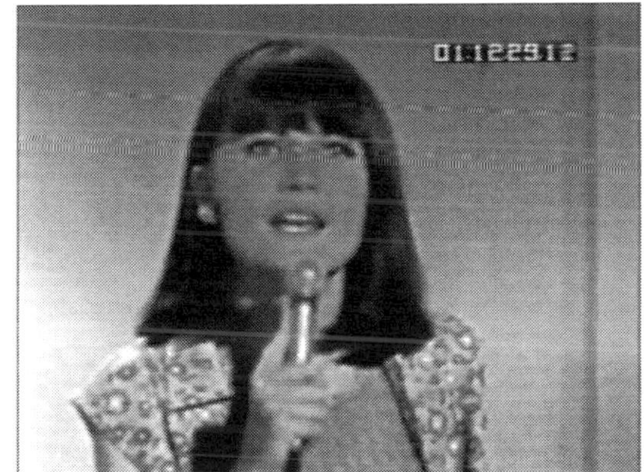

L-R: Billy J. Kramer with The Dakotas; Dave Berry; Ian Whitcomb; Sandle Shaw, The Barron Knights; Twinkle

Episode 85: 8th January 1966

Opening Medley: **Jackie DeShannon** - C.C. Rider / **Bobby Sherman** and **Dick and Dee Dee** - Reelin' And Rockin' / **Billy Preston** and **The Knickerbockers** - Jenny, Jenny (End of Medley)
Dick and Dee Dee - Lightnin' Strikes
The Blossoms - Good Good Lovin'
Jackie DeShannon - We Can Work It Out
The Knickerbockers - Lies
Bobby Sherman - Michelle (with Jackie DeShannon cameo)
The Knickerbockers - Let Me Be
Jackie DeShannon - As Tears Go By
The Wellingtons - Flowers On The Wall
Dick and Dee Dee - Don't Think Twice, It's Alright
Billy Preston - Uptight
Closing Medley: **The Knickerbockers** - CC Rider / **Billy Preston**, **Bobby Sherman** and **Jackie DeShannon** - Jenny, Jenny / **Dick and Dee Dee** - CC Rider

DICK AND DEE DEE: 'Lightnin' Strikes' was a current hit for Lou Christie.

THE KNICKERBOCKERS: Beau Charles (Robert Cecchino, guitar and vocals), John Charles (bass and vocals), Buddy Randell (William Crandall, d. 1998 - vocals and saxophone) and Jimmy Walker (d. 2020 - drums and vocals). Pop and Garage band from Bergenfield, New Jersey. The Beatle-esque 'Lies' was a No. 20 US hit.

JACKIE DESHANNON: Someone who was on the very first Pilot show almost 3 years earlier, it is only right that Jackie DeShannon was also present for the show's swansong.

While not quite an out and out classic, the last show was at least filmed 100% in the 'Shindig!' studios, and is close to the spirit of the early Jack Good-produced shows. Incidentally, the reason Dick and Dee Dee are wearing daft costumes is to promote 'Batman', one of several forthcoming TV shows that would replace 'Shindig!'. Rival shows 'Hullabaloo', 'Shivaree' and 'Hollywood A Go-Go' would also be finished by April, as would the UK's 'Ready, Steady, Go!' and 'Thank Your Lucky Stars' before the year was over.

L-R: Dick and Dee Dee; The Blossoms; The Knickerbockers; Jackie DeShannon; The Wellingtons; Billy Preston

RHINO OFFICIAL VHS RELEASES (1991-1992)

Shindig! Presents The Righteous Brothers
Rhino Home Video - RNVD 1450

Unchained Melody
You've Lost That Lovin' Feelin'
Little Latin Lupe Lu
Just Once In My Life
Justine
Night Time Is The Right Time
Ko Ko Joe
Great Gettin' Up Morning

Shindig! Presents Motor City Magic
Rhino Home Video - RNVD 1451

Junior Walker and The All Stars - Shotgun
Mary Wells - My Guy
Marvin Gaye - How Sweet It Is
The Blossoms - Dancing In The Streets
The Temptations - My Girl
The Supremes - Stop! In The Name Of Love
The Four Tops - It's The Same Old Song
Martha and The Vandellas - Nowhere To Run
Smokey Robinson and The Miracles - You've Really Got A Hold Of Me
Marvin Gaye - Can I Get A Witness

Shindig! Presents Frat Party
Rhino Home Video - RNVD 1452

The Kingsmen - Louie Louie
The Sir Douglas Quintet - She's About A Mover
Roy Head - Treat Her Right
The Olympics - Good Lovin'
Dobie Gray - The 'In' Crowd
The Hondells - Little Honda
The McCoys - Hang On Sloopy
The Righteous Brothers - Let The Good Times Roll
Zsa Zsa Gabor - High Heel Sneakers
The Isley Brothers - Shout
Jerry Lee Lewis - Great Balls Of Fire

Shindig! Presents Legends Of Rock 'N' Roll
Rhino Home Video - RNVD 1453

The Righteous Brothers - Ko Ko Joe
Jerry Lee Lewis - High School Confidential
Aretha Franklin - Mockingbird
Tina Turner - Goodbye, So Long
Bo Diddley - Hey Bo Diddley
Little Anthony and The Imperials - Hurt So Bad
Johnny Cash - Orange Blossom Special
The Everly Brothers - Wake Up Little Susie
Chuck Berry - Back In The U.S.A.
James Brown - Night Train

Shindig! Presents British Invasion Vol. 1
Rhino Home Video - RNVD 1454

Gerry and The Pacemakers - Don't Let The Sun Catch You Crying
Herman's Hermits - I'm Into Something Good
Billy J. Kramer with The Dakotas - Little Children
Manfred Mann - Doo Wah Diddy
The Searchers - Needles and Pins
The Nashville Teens - Tobacco Road
The Honeycombs - Have I The Right
Ian Whitcomb - You Turn Me On
Peter and Gordon - A World Without Love
Freddy & The Dreamers - I'm Telling You Now

Shindig! Presents Sixties Superstars
Rhino Home Video - RNVD 1455

The Mamas and Papas - California Dreamin'
The Byrds - Turn! Turn! Turn!
Donovan - Catch The Wind
The Turtles - Let Me Be
Beau Brummels - Laugh Laugh
The Yardbirds - For Your Love
Donovan - Colours
The Turtles - It Ain't Me Babe
The Byrds - Feel A Whole Lot Better
The Gentrys - Keep On Dancing

Shindig! Presents Soul
Rhino Home Video - RNVD 1456

James Brown - Papa's Got A Brand New Bag
James Brown - Please, Please, Please
Joe Tex - Hold What You've Got
Booker T. & The M.G's - Green Onions
Marvin Gaye - Hitch Hike
Tina Turner and Marvin Gaye - Money/I'll Be Doggone
Major Lance - Monkey Time
Aretha Franklin - Rock-A-Bye Your Baby
Tina Turner - A Fool In Love

Shindig! Presents Groovy Gals
Rhino Home Video - RNVD 1457

Ketty Lester - Love Letters
Aretha Franklin - Shoop Shoop Song
Lesley Gore - Judy's Turn To Cry
The Toys - Lover's Concerto
Fontella Bass - Rescue Me
The Supremes - Baby Love
The Shangri-Las - Give Him A Great Big Kiss
Petula Clark - Downtown
The Blossoms - I Like It Like That
Tina Turner - Ooh Poo-Pah-Do
Jackie DeShannon - What The World Needs Now

Shindig! Presents Jerry Lee Lewis
Rhino Home Video - RNVD 1458

Mean Woman Blues
High School Confidential
Great Balls Of Fire
Long Tall Sally
I Believe In You
Whole Lotta Shakin' Going On [with Jackie Sedaka]
Rockin' Pneumonia and The Boogie Woogie Flu
Breathless
Take Me Out To The Ballgame [with Neil Sedaka]

Shindig! Presents The Kinks
Rhino Home Video - RNVD 1459

You Really Got Me
Set Me Free
See My Friends
Tired Of Waiting For You
All Day and All Of The Night
Who'll Be The Next In Line
I'm A Lover Not A Fighter
Long Tall Shorty
I Gotta Move

Shindig! Presents British Invasion Vol. 2
Rhino Home Video - RNVD 1460

Herman's Hermits - Can't You Hear My Heart Beat
Peter and Gordon - I Go To Pieces
Billy J. Kramer with The Dakotas - Trains and Boats and Planes
Freddy and The Dreamers - You Were Made For Me
The Yardbirds - Heart Full Of Soul
The Zombies - Tell Her No
The Animals - We Gotta Get Outta This Place
Gerry and The Pacemakers - Ferry Cross The Mersey
Chad and Jeremy - Willow Weep For Me
Manfred Mann - Sha La La

Shindig! Presents Jackie Wilson
Rhino Home Video - RNVD 1461

That's Why I Love You So
Sing
Danny Boy
I'm So Lonely
Whole Lotta Shakin' Going On [with Jerry Lee Lewis]
I Believe I'll Love On
No Pity (In The Naked City)
Baby Workout
She's Alright

ARTISTS' EPISODE APPEARANCE LISTING

Jewel Akens - 23, 28
Steve Alaimo - 24
Terry Allen - 47
John Andrea - 21, 22, 23, 26, 27, 29, 30, 46, 51
The Angels - Pilot #3
The Animals - 60, 75
The Apollas - 9
Louis Armstrong - 66, 68
The Brian Auger Trinity - 75
The Barbarians - 25
Susan Barrett - 21
The Barron Knights - 84
Len Barry - 71, 72
Fontella Bass - 67
Shirley Bassey - 83
The Beach Boys - 16, 32
The Beatles - 4
The Beau Brummels - 27, 44
Cliff Bennett and The Rebel Rousers - 40
Pamela Bennett - 2
Tony Bennett - 27
Chuck Berry - 29
Dave Berry - 26, 41, 46, 84
John Bill - 3
The Bitter End Singers - 40
Cilla Black - 32
Terry Black - 44, 46
The Blossoms - Pilot #3, 1, 2, 3, 6, 7, 11, 13, 15, 17, 18, 19, 21, 22, 23, 24, 28, 29, 30, 31, 33, 34, 35, 36, 37, 38, 39, 41, 42, 43, 44, 45, 46, 48, 49, 51, 53, 54, 56, 57, 58, 59, 60, 62, 63, 64, 65, 72, 74, 78, 82, 85
The Graham Bond Organisation - 76
Booker T. and The M.G.'s - 50
Jimmy Boyd - 34
Delaney Bramlett - Pilot #3, 2, 29, 34, 35, 37, 38, 53, 56
Elkie Brooks - 5, 78
James Brown - 50
Jewel Brown - 66, 68
James Burton - 31, 53, 72
The Byrds - 41, 52, 63
The Cables - 2
Glen Campbell - Pilot #1, 8, 20, 21, 22, 24, 25, 28, 30, 31, 34, 36, 39, 42, 48, 49, 50, 59, 61, 63, 64, 72
Freddy Cannon - 13
Linda Carr - 38, 46
Johnny Cash - Pilot #2, 19
Ted Cassidy - 65
Chad and Jeremy - 12, 42
Chad and Jill - 52
George Chakiris - 79, 83
The Chambers Brothers - Pilot #1, 6, 13, 26, 34
Gene Chandler - 51
The Chaps - Pilot #1
Ray Charles - 36
Chubby Checker - 14
The Chiffons - 45
Jimmy Clanton - 30, 39
The Dave Clark Five - 15, 20, 46, 53, 62, 80
Linda Clark - 47
Petula Clark - 20, 40
Roy Clark - Pilot #2, 26, 46
Mike Clifford - 46, 54
The Coasters - 23
Jerry Cole - 2, 3, 24, 26, 29, 42
Jesse Collins - Pilot #1
The Collins Kids- Pilot #2, 51
The Condors - 22
Sam Cooke - 1
Joey Cooper - 25, 29, 32, 34, 37, 38, 53, 56, 63
Lyn Cornell - 4
Chris Crosby - Pilot #2, 7
Vic Dana - 17, 24
Carolyn Daye - 11
The Karl Denver Trio - 4
Jackie DeShannon - Pilot #1, 37, 49, 53, 59, 85
Dino, Desi and Billy - 35
The Detergents - 19
Dick and Dee Dee - 7, 19, 28, 32, 33, 35, 40, 49, 55, 58, 59, 85
Bo Diddley - 49
The Dixie Cups - 14, 47
Donovan - 48, 56
Bobby Doqui and Arnold Rollin - 10

OTHER BOOKS BY PETER CHECKSFIELD

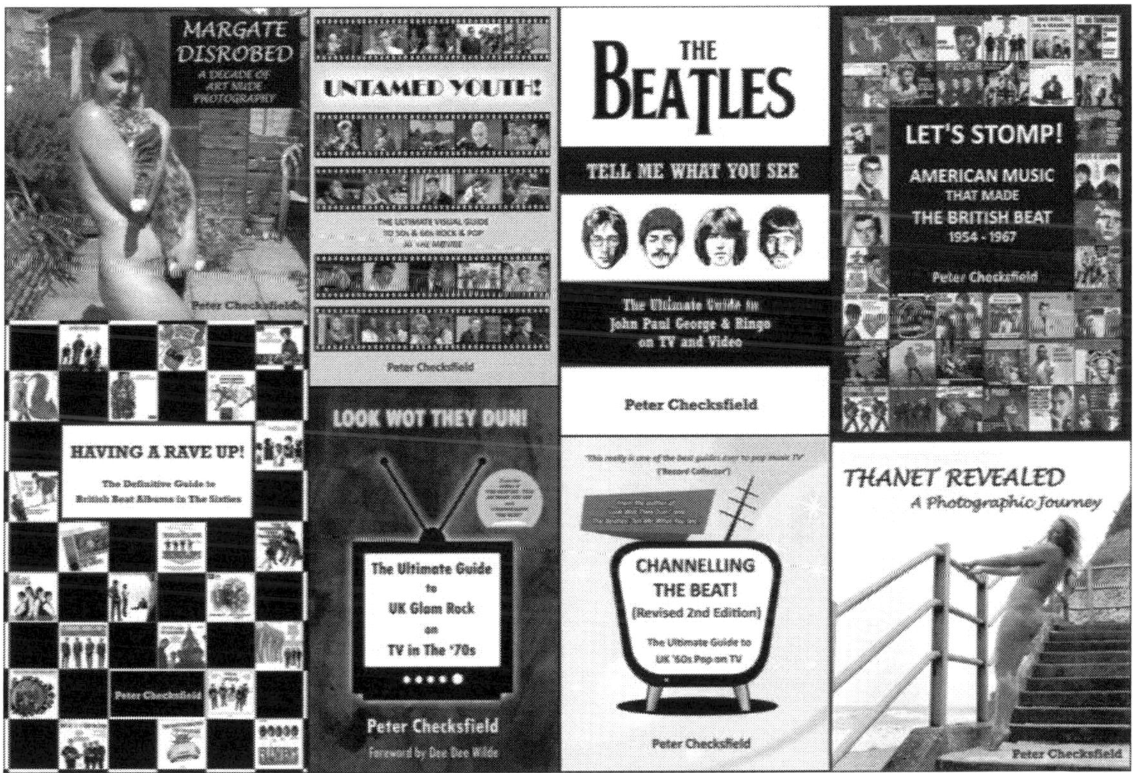

See www.peterchecksfield.com for more details!

ABOUT THE AUTHOR

An acknowledged expert in his field, Peter Checksfield is the author of six other acclaimed books on music, as well as two books of art-nude photography. He has also contributed to 'Record Collector', 'Now Dig This', 'Fire-Ball Mail', and various website and blogs. His interests include collecting rare music TV footage, walking, cycling and local history. He lives on the Kent coast in the UK with his partner Heather.

Made in the USA
Middletown, DE
04 November 2021